Keeping Good Company

A Season-by-Season Collection of Recipes, with Entertaining and Homemaking Ideas

Recipes by Roxie Kelley and Friends

Illustrations by Shelly Reeves Smith

Andrews McMeel
Publishing, LLC

Kansas City

07 08 09 10 11 WKT 10 9 8 7 6 5 4 3

ISBN-13: 978-0-7407-6535-3

ISBN-10: 0-7407-6535-3

Library of Congress Control Number: 2006938403

www.andrewsmcmeel.com

ATTENTION: SCHOOLS AND BUSINESSES
Andrews McMeel books are available at quantity discounts with bulk purchase for educational, business, or sales promotional use. For information, please write to: Special Sales Department, Andrews McMeel Publishing, LLC, 4520 Main Street, Kansas City, Missouri 64111.

Presented To:

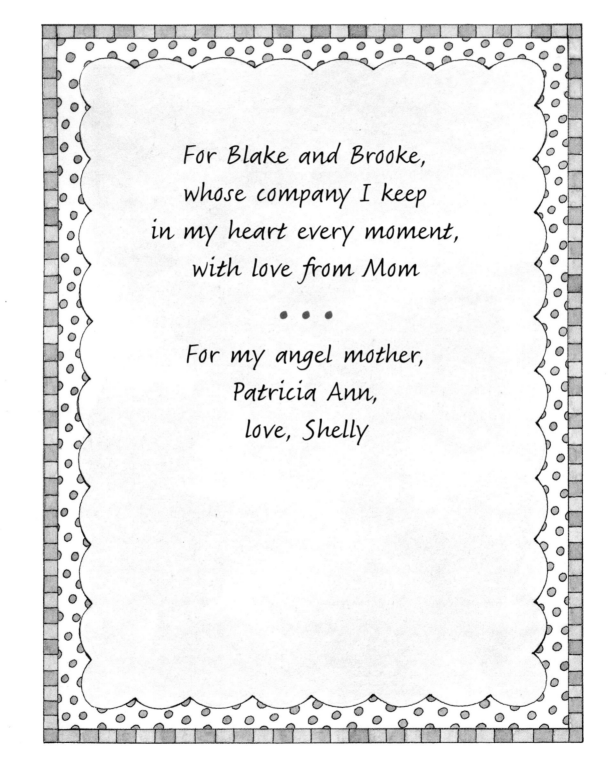

For Blake and Brooke,
whose company I keep
in my heart every moment,
with love from Mom

• • •

For my angel mother,
Patricia Ann,
love, Shelly

Table of Contents

Spring

Summer

Autumn

Winter

Morning, Noon, and Night

Dear Friends,

What a pleasure and privilege it is for us to share another fun-filled book! Following in the same style as our previous books, we always like to say this is designed to be more than a cookbook. Because we are more than empty food vessels perpetually needing to be refilled, we all long for an occasional guide to addressing our other human needs—those of companionship and connection. Keeping Good Company is a reminder, both in name and content, that it is the good company of friends and family that feeds and sustains us, as well as the favorite foods we share.

Keeping Good Company also happens to be the name of our gift shop located in scenic Lake of the Ozarks. One of our goals while you are visiting our store is to entertain all five of your senses, in a very balanced and relaxing way. With this as one of your objectives within your own home, you will find it easier to create an atmosphere that is memorable, enjoyable, and comfortable, not only for your guests and family but for yourself as well.

Nothing appeals to the senses like changing weather and the different times of the year. This seasonal format is our choice for this volume. We hope through Shelly's graceful hand this book becomes a reminder of the blessings each season has to offer us.

Enjoy!

Roxie Kelley and
Shelly Reeves Smith

"Where we love is home, home that our feet may leave, but not our hearts..."

— Oliver Wendell Holmes

SPRING

Keepsakes...

BULBS!

HYACINTH

DAFFODIL

HANDS TO WORK

Keep a garden Journal...

BUZZ... BUZZ...

SPRING

CROCUS

FEVER!

"Another of life's ironies
is to have house cleaning,
gardening, and spring fever
all come at the same time."

Unknown

Spring Spread

This light cream cheese spread is wonderful on bagels or as a spread on miniature party sandwiches...

Lily of the Valley

Combine 8 oz. cream cheese with:

¼ cup peeled and grated carrots
1 green onion, sliced thin
1 celery stalk, sliced thin
½ tsp. seasoned salt

Chill until ready to use.

Ranch
AVOCADO DIP

This mildly flavored dip can be used with our Southwest Chicken Eggroll Recipe, or as a wonderful condiment with stuffed baked potatoes or raw vegetables.

1 ripe avocado, peeled & diced
1 tsp. lemon juice
16 oz. sour cream
Ranch dip mix

Mash diced avocado with lemon juice until smooth and creamy. Prepare dip mix with sour cream. Fold avocado mixture into ranch dip. Chill 1 hour before serving.

Makes about 3 cups.

Southwest Chicken Eggrolls

One of my good friends, Paula, is to blame for this recipe. She introduced me to a similar appetizer at a well-known chain restaurant, and I couldn't quit thinking about them for weeks. Each time I ordered these eggrolls, I would scribble probable ingredients on my napkin, filing each one away until I was confident enough to make them on my own at home. So that you won't have a filing cabinet full of splotchy paper napkins, here is my version.

1 small onion, peeled and chopped
¼ cup butter or cooking oil
1 clove garlic, crushed
1 (10 oz.) pkg. frozen chopped spinach, thawed and squeezed dry
2 chicken breasts, cooked and chopped
½ cup frozen corn

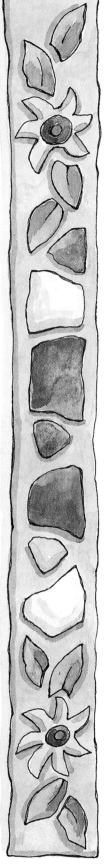

½ cup cooked black beans
½ to 1 tsp. ground red pepper
¼ tsp. ground oregano
¼ cup fresh cilantro
(or 1 tsp. dried crushed Cilantro)
1 cup salsa
1 tsp. cornstarch
1 (4 oz.) can chopped green chiles

egg roll wrappers
vegetable oil for frying

1 Recipe Ranch Avacado Dip

Sauté onion in butter, along with garlic, until clear. Add remaining 10 ingredients and heat through slowly. Following the directions on the eggroll package, fill wrappers with chicken filling and deep fry in vegetable oil until golden brown. Remove and drain. Serve immediately with Ranch Avacado Dip.

Makes about 10 eggrolls.

Cucumbers with Dressing

Pretty, cool, and by far, the best cucumber salad I've ever had!

1 cup mayonnaise
1/4 cup sugar
1/4 cup vinegar
salt and pepper to taste
4 cups sliced cucumbers
1 pint cherry tomatoes,
sliced in half

In a bowl, combine mayonnaise, sugar, vinegar, salt, and pepper. Add cucumbers and tomatoes; stir to coat. Cover and refrigerate at least 2 hours. Makes 8~10 servings.

Charlie's PASTA SALAD

Charlie received this recipe from a good friend in St. Louis. Best when prepared a day ahead, it serves a crowd and always gets rave reviews.

1 medium cucumber, finely chopped
1 medium red onion, finely chopped
½ cup vinegar (apple cider vinegar is good)
1 cup sugar
1 Tbsp. dry mustard
1 tsp. salt
1 tsp. garlic powder
1 tsp. pepper
1 Tbsp. dried parsley

Combine these ingredients.

1 small jar pimiento
1 green pepper, chopped
1 can pitted black olives, sliced
1 jar marinated artichoke hearts, drained
1 pkg. sliced pepperoni (optional)
1 lb. pkg. shell pasta, cooked according to package directions, and drained

Then add these and chill.

"Charlie... thanks for a friendship that grows sweeter with each passing year!"

Raspberry Poppy Seed
DRESSING

This recipe comes from Mike and Cheryl Castle, the owners of On the Rise Bakery and Bistro in Osage Beach, MO. In addition to a bountiful assortment of bakery goods, this charming establishment will astound you with a lunch you'll not soon forget.

Combine the following ingredients in a blender and mix well:

2 cups mayonnaise
1/3 cup Half-n-Half
2 T. poppy seeds
2/3 cup sugar
1/2 cup raspberry vinegar
3 T. raspberry jam

Keeps in the refrigerator for 1 week.

Serves about 8.

Strawberry & Romaine Salad

Another treat from On the Rise; you'll love this salad with Raspberry-Poppyseed Dressing.

2 heads romaine lettuce, washed and dried and torn into pieces
1 pint fresh strawberries, sliced
1 red onion, peeled and sliced thin
½ cup toasted, slivered almonds

Toss romaine, onions and dressing together. Top with strawberries and almonds. Serves 4-6.

New Potatoes in Sour Cream

I never tire of potatoes! This is an easy dish that can be served hot or cold.

1 cup butter, melted
10-12 small red potatoes, scrubbed clean
2/3 cup sour cream
2 Tbsp. snipped chives (or 2 Tbsp. dried dill weed)
8 slices bacon, cooked crisp and crumbled
salt and pepper to taste

Slice unpeeled potatoes (think thin!) and cook in butter over low heat until tender for 15-20 minutes, stirring occasionally. Add bacon, chives, seasonings, and sour cream. Heat slowly for one minute more ~ do not boil or sour cream will curdle. Serves 4.

Honey Baked Beans

Maybe this is a sign of getting older, but in the spring my thoughts turn to

Barbecue!

Add this delicious side dish to your next cookout. Combine the following ingredients in a saucepan and cook on low for 30-45 minutes.

2 (16- or 21-ounce) cans baked beans in sauce
3/4 cup barbecue sauce
2 Tbsp. chopped onion
4 slices bacon, crisp-cooked
and crumbled
2 Tbsp. honey
3/4 tsp. paprika
1/4 tsp. dry mustard

Chicken Pasta Soup

Don't let the length of this recipe intimidate you ~ it's really very easy and well worth the effort! ♥

6-8 chicken breast tenders
½ tsp. seasoned salt
4 Tbsp. olive oil
½ cup butter, divided in half
1 small onion, diced
2 stalks celery, sliced thin, crosswise
1 carrot, peeled and shredded
½ cup flour
2 (14 oz.) cans chicken broth
ground red pepper to taste
  (start out with a moderate amount!)
freshly ground white or black pepper to taste
¼ tsp. dried basil
2 cups half and half
4 oz. sliced fresh mushrooms
1 cup sugar snap peas
1 Tbsp. sugar
6-8 oz. penne pasta

Sprinkle chicken with seasoned salt. Sauté in olive oil over medium heat in large skillet about 6 minutes per side or until done. Remove chicken and set aside to cool. In the same pan, melt 1/4 cup butter. Over medium heat, cook onion, celery, and carrot until limp. Add flour, stirring until smooth. Gradually add chicken broth, stirring constantly. Turn heat to low. Slice chicken diagonally into thin pieces. Add to broth with ground peppers and basil. Slowly add half-and-half. Stir and heat through.

Melt remaining 1/4 cup butter in a large shallow bowl in the microwave. Combine mushrooms, snap peas, and sugar with butter and cook on high for 3 minutes, stirring once midway. Fold this into soup mixture on the stove and simmer for about 10 minutes. Meanwhile prepare pasta according to package directions. Drain well and add immediately to soup. A complete meal when served with hot, crusty bread. Serves 10-12.

Tex-Mex Chicken Soup

I Love this soup - not only because of its unsurpassed blend of flavors, but because it is also very low in fat.

½ pkg. chili mix
4-6 boneless chicken breasts
1 tsp. vegetable oil
cooking spray
1 onion, chopped
¾ cup thinly sliced yellow
  bell pepper

¾ cup thinly sliced
  red bell pepper
2 cups chicken broth
2 cups water
salt and pepper
  to taste
½ cup bottled salsa

1 Tbsp. fresh lime juice

3 (10-in.) flour tortillas, cut into ¼-inch-thick strips
¾ cup shredded reduced-fat Monterey Jack cheese

Sprinkle chili mix into a shallow bowl and dredge chicken in it. Heat vegetable oil with some cooking spray in a large skillet over medium-high heat. Add the chicken and sauté 6 minutes on each side or until chicken is done. Remove chicken from pan and cool. Slice chicken on the diagonal into thin slices and set aside. Add onion and peppers to skillet and sauté for 3 minutes. Add chicken slices, broth, water, salt, and pepper. Bring to a boil. Simmer about 30 minutes. Add salsa and lime juice and simmer an additional 10 minutes. Preheat broiler. Spread the tortilla strips in a single layer on a baking sheet coated with cooking spray; lightly coat tortillas with cooking spray. Broil strips for 3-4 minutes until lightly browned, stirring once. Ladle soup into bowls, top with tortilla strips, and sprinkle with cheese. Serves 6-8.

Cream of Anything Soup

In only about 30 minutes you can prepare this elegant and easy soup. The bonus is it's low in fat as well as very satisfying.

8 cups vegetables (such as carrots, broccoli and
    mushrooms), cut into ½-inch pieces
2 large potatoes, peeled and cut into ½-inch pieces
1 onion, peeled and sliced
2 cloves garlic, minced
2 tsp. salt
freshly ground pepper to taste
4 cups water
2 cups milk
snipped chives for garnish

In a large soup pot, cook vegetables, potatoes, onion, garlic, salt, and pepper in about 4 cups water until very tender, (about 20-25 minutes). Spoon ¼ of mixture into blender or food processor. Cover and blend until smooth. Repeat three times with remaining mixture until all is blended. Pour soup back in pot. Stir in milk. Heat through and ladle into bowls. Garnish with chives.

Serves 4-6.

Lemon-Herb Grilled Chicken

½ cup vegetable oil
⅓ cup lemon juice
2 Tbsp. honey
1 tsp. dried rosemary
½ tsp. poultry seasoning
salt and pepper to taste
2 cloves garlic, crushed
4-6 split chicken breasts
lemon wedges

Combine all ingredients except chicken and mix well. Place chicken in a heavy zip-top plastic bag, and pour oil mixture over it. Seal bag, and marinate chicken in refrigerator 8 hours or overnight. Drain and discard marinade. Cook chicken, covered with grill lid, over medium-hot coals about 30-35 minutes, turning occasionally. Garnish with lemon wedges.

Makes 4-6 servings.

Grilled Honey-Garlic Chops

4 center-cut boneless pork chops,
  1½-inches-thick
¼ cup lemon juice
¼ cup honey
2 Tbsp. soy sauce
1 Tbsp. water
2 cloves garlic, minced

Combine the five marinade ingredients and pour over pork chops in a heavy zip-top bag. Place in a large shallow bowl (in case of leakage) and refrigerate for at least 4 hours. Remove chops from marinade and grill over medium-hot coals about 15 minutes or until internal temperature is 150°. Turn once during grilling.
Serves 4.

Great with "Garlic Smashed Potatoes" and Applesauce!

This-Could-Be-Love...
MUFFINS

A muffin so rich and dreamy,
you'll think it's dessert.

¼ cup butter, melted
¼ cup cocoa
2 eggs, lightly beaten
1 cup sugar
1 tsp. vanilla
1 cup flour
½ tsp. ground cinnamon
1 tsp. baking powder
¼ cup chopped pecans, optional

1 chocolate bar (any variety) chopped

Combine eggs, sugar and vanilla in a mixing bowl. Add melted butter, cocoa, flour, cinnamon, baking powder, and pecans and mix just until blended. Place paper baking cups in a muffin pan, and coat lightly with cooling spray. Spoon batter into cups, filling each ⅔ full. Sprinkle with chocolate pieces. Bake at 350° for about 20 minutes, until sides pull away from paper and tops are dried to touch. Remove from pans to cool.

Makes about 10 muffins.

Big Bird Bread Sticks

These seed-sprinkled semi-soft bread sticks (say that ten times!) are a quick complement to any soup or salad.

1 package refrigerator crescent-roll dough
vegetable oil spray
poppy seeds
sesame seeds
sea salt or margarita salt
dried onion (optional)

Preheat oven to 350°. Lightly spray cookie sheet with vegetable oil spray. Lay crescent-roll dough out in one large single layer on cookie sheet, pressing all perforated edges together to seal. Spray surface of dough with vegetable oil spray. Sprinkle both kinds of seeds over entire surface of dough. Then sprinkle with salt and onion, less generously than with seeds.

Bake 10-15 minutes or until golden brown. Remove from oven and cut into sticks about 1" wide and 3" long. (A pizza cutting wheel is handy here!) Serves 6-8.

Garden Muffins

4 cups flour
2½ cups sugar
4 tsp. baking soda
½ tsp. nutmeg
4 tsp. cinnamon
1 tsp. salt
2 cups grated carrots
2 cups grated zucchini
1 cup chopped pecans
1 cup coconut
2 tart apples, peeled and grated
6 eggs (or egg equivalent)
1 cup vegetable oil
1 cup buttermilk
2 tsp. vanilla

Preheat oven to 375°. In a large bowl, sift together the flour, sugar, baking soda, nutmeg, cinnamon, and salt. Stir in carrots, zucchini, pecans, coconut, and apples. In smaller bowl, whisk together the remaining ingredients and add to the flour and vegetable mixture. Stir until blended. Spoon batter into greased or paper-lined muffin tins, filling each cup ⅔ full. Bake 22-28 minutes, or until muffins spring back when touched. Cool for 5 minutes before removing from pan. Makes about 2 dozen.

Chocolate Chip Banana Bread

~Beat first six ingredients together until blended.

½ cup butter, room temperature
1¼ cups sugar
2 eggs
½ cup sour cream
1 tsp. vanilla
1 cup mashed ripe bananas

~ Stir in the dry indredients and chocolate chips until moistened.

1¾ cups flour
1 tsp. baking soda
1 tsp. baking powder
pinch of salt
¾ cup semisweet chocolate chips

~ Divide batter between two greased loaf pans. Bake at 325° for about 40-50 minutes, or until tester comes out clean. Cool in pan for 15 minutes and then remove to rack to cool completely. When cool, drizzle with glaze.

~ Chocolate Glaze:
½ cup semisweet chocolate chips
3 Tbsp. butter

In a heavy zip-top bag, heat chocolate chips and butter together in microwave 35-40 seconds. "Massage" bag until ingredients are well blended. Snip off bottom corner and drizzle over each loaf.

Banana-Brownie Pie

- ¼ cup butter
- 3 oz. cream cheese, softened
- 1½ cups sifted powdered sugar
- ¼ cup whipping cream
- ½ tsp. vanilla
- 3 bananas, sliced
- 1 (6 oz.) can pineapple juice
- 4 brownies, cut into 1" pieces
- 1 baked 9-inch pastry shell
- ½ cup chopped pecans
- ¼ cup semisweet chocolate chips
- 8 oz. whipped topping or whipped cream for garnish

Serves 6-8.

Beat butter and cream cheese together until creamy; gradually add powdered sugar alternately with whipping cream. Stir in vanilla. Set this filling aside.

Toss banana slices in pineapple juice; drain. Pat slices dry with paper towels.

Spoon half of filling into baked pastry shell. Arrange banana slices on filling. Add a layer of brownie pieces. Top with remaining filling, and sprinkle with pecans. Set aside. Melt chocolate in a heavy zip-top bag in the microwave. Heat 35-40 seconds at a time and "massage" bag until completely melted. Snip off bottom corner of bag and drizzle chocolate over pecans on top of pie. Spoon (or pipe from zip-top bag) dollops of whipped topping around outside edge of pie.

Chocolate Dessert Cups

Bring smiles to your springtime table with these chocolate dessert cups...

They are as much fun to look at as they are to eat. Fill them with anything from jellybeans to ice cream. Simply follow the directions on the label for melting an 8-ounce package of semi-sweet or white chocolate chips. With the back of a spoon, spread melted chocolate over the inside of 10 foil or double-layered paper baking cups, coating the entire surface. Place cups in muffin pan and refrigerate until firm, (about 1 hour).

Hint: Cool your hands under cold water before handling to remove foil from chocolate.

German Chocolate Cheesecake Bars

This elegant dessert would be perfect for your Valentine ♥, but also more than appropriate year-round when a light (but luscious!) treat is in order.

- 1½ cups graham cracker or Oreo cookie crumbs
- ¼ cup sugar
- 5 Tbsp. butter, melted
- 2 (8 oz.) pkgs. cream cheese, room temperature
- 1 (14 oz) can creamy chocolate Eagle Brand sweetened condensed milk
- 3 eggs
- 3 Tbsp. cornstarch
- 1 tsp. vanilla
- 1 cup chopped pecans
- 1 cup sweetened flaked coconut
- ½ to ¾ cup caramel ice cream topping
- chocolate bar, shaved into "curls" using a vegetable peeler
- powdered sugar

Preheat oven to 325°. Combine the first three ingredients in a medium-sized mixing bowl. Then press evenly into the bottom of a 9" x 13" baking pan. In a separate bowl, beat cream cheese until smooth. Add Eagle Brand, eggs, cornstarch, and vanilla, and beat for 2 minutes. Pour batter over the top of crust. Sprinkle with chopped pecans. Bake for 15 minutes. Remove pan from oven. Increase oven temperature to 350°. Sprinkle top of cheesecake bars with coconut and return to oven for 10-12 minutes, or until coconut is golden brown. Remove from oven and cool. Drizzle caramel ice cream topping evenly over the top of bars. Garnish with chocolate curls and dust with powdered sugar. Refrigerate until ready to serve. Cut into diamond-shaped bars. Makes about 10-12 servings.

Gooey Butter Cookies

St. Louis natives like to claim Gooey Butter Cake as a St. Louis specialty.

My neighbor Anne Wall also hails from St. Louis, and she knew my Cardinal-lovin' heart would skip a beat at the thought of a COOKIE that tasted like Gooey Butter Cake!

...Here is her rich and dreamy recipe.

½ cup butter

¼ tsp. vanilla
1 egg
1 (8 oz.) pkg. cream cheese
1 (1 lb. 2.25 oz.) box butter recipe cake mix
powdered sugar for dipping
cooking spray

Beat butter, vanilla, egg, and cream cheese until light and fluffy. Mix in dry cake mix. Chill for 30 minutes. Preheat oven to 350°. Lightly coat cookie sheet with cooking spray. Drop by teaspoonfuls in a bowl of powdered sugar; roll into balls. Bake 10-12 minutes.

Makes 3-4 dozen

Raspberry Tart

A prepared pie crust turns this recipe into elegance in short order.

Preheat oven to 450°.

Press prepared pie crust into a large tart pan (or several small pans). Prick bottom with a fork and partially bake for 10 minutes. Remove from oven and reduce temperature to 325°.

Filling:

- 3 (8 oz.) packages cream cheese, room temperature
- 3/4 cup sugar
- 4 eggs, room temperature
- 1/4 cup fresh lemon juice
- 2 tsp. pure lemon extract

Raspberry Topping:

- 24 oz. frozen unsweetened raspberries, thawed and drained, reserving juice
- 1 cup sugar
- 1/4 cup cornstarch
- lemon zest for garnish

Mix together the cream cheese and sugar until smooth. Add eggs, one at a time. Add lemon juice and extract and beat 2 minutes. Pour into partially baked crust. Bake at 325° for 15 minutes. Leave tart in oven with oven off for 15 minutes longer. Chill for 2 hours.

Prepare topping by mixing sugar with cornstarch in saucepan. Add reserved juice and mix with whisk on medium-high heat until mixture comes to a boil. Lower heat, stirring until slightly thickened (about 2 or 3 minutes). Fold in fruit. Cool and store topping in refrigerator until ready to serve. When ready to serve, spoon topping over each slice and garnish with lemon zest if desired.

Serves 6-8.

CHOCOLATE HEARTS

Tuck these little treasures next to a scoop of ice cream or a dish of chocolate pudding to make dessert memorable and fun!

· 4 oz. semisweet or dark chocolate
· 2 oz. white chocolate (optional)
· candy sprinkles, if desired
· small heart-shaped cookie cutter

Place water in the bottom of a double boiler so that it comes to within ½ inch of the upper pan (water should not touch the upper pan). Chop 4 oz. dark chocolate and put in the upper pan. Place double boiler over low heat. Stir constantly until melted and smooth. Spread chocolate evenly onto a baking sheet lined with waxed paper to about ⅛-inch thickness. Top with candy sprinkles, if desired. Allow the chocolate to stand until almost dry.

Firmly press a small heart-shaped cookie cutter into the chocolate. Allow the chocolate to set up. Then carefully slide each heart off the waxed paper. Hearts can be decorated with melted chocolate (dots, stripes, swirls, etc.) if desired.

Makes about a dozen hearts.

Angels Among Us Cake

Imagine a teacher who has such rapport with children that her presence alone can turn a classroom of rowdy second graders into a band of heavenly angels. In our community, that teacher is Donna Flory.

Mrs. Flory has established a tradition of inviting parents into her classroom late in the spring to be part of a year-end celebration. The atmosphere is one of respect and gratitude. Lots of friends contribute to the entertainment. Then all the children in the class join in singing Mrs. Flory's version of "Angels Among Us", their voices light as gossamer wings. They pull their handmade halos out of their desks on the last verse, and hold them above their little heads. Tears well up in the parents' eyes and throats tighten as we all take in the extreme brevity of this golden moment. It's difficult to tell who is honoring whom at this celebration (which is the way life should be lived, isn't it?) We only know that love is in the room and that someday Mrs. Flory will surely have a special place in heaven. This recipe was created as a tribute to her. It is a labor of love but fully worth the effort.

- 10 large eggs
- 1½ cups sifted powdered sugar
- 1 cup sifted cake flour
- 1½ tsp. cream of tartar
- 1 tsp. vanilla
- 1 cup sugar

While they are cold, separate eggs, one at a time, placing egg whites in a large grease-free mixing bowl, and egg yolks in a smaller bowl. Let egg whites stand at room temperature for 30 minutes. Be sure that no part of the egg yolk gets mixed in with the whites (this is important!) Sift powdered sugar and flour together 3 times and set aside. ♡♡ Add cream of tartar and vanilla to egg whites. With an electric mixture on medium speed, beat until soft peaks form (tips curl). Gradually add granulated sugar, 2 tablespoons at a time, beating until stiff peaks form (tips stand up straight). ♡♡ Sift a quarter of the dry mixture over the beaten egg whites; gently fold in. Repeat, folding in remaining dry mixture by fourths. Pour into ungreased 10" tube pan. With a narrow metal spatula, gently cut through the batter to remove any air pockets. Bake on lowest rack for 40-45 minutes or until top springs back when lightly touched. Immediately invert cake: cool at least 30 minutes. Loosen sides of cake from pan with narrow metal spatula: remove cake.

Tips for A+ Angel Food Cakes

1. Just one speck of egg yolk or any other fat can compromise the beating quality of egg whites.

2. Don't over or underbeat the egg whites. They should be stiff but not dry or your cake will fall.

3. Make sure bowl, beaters and pan are grease-free before starting.

Makes 12-15 servings

Red Cake

Dee Stoelting has a reputation for being one of the best cooks in our community. She and her sister, Chris, share this family recipe.

3/4 cup vegetable oil
1½ cups sugar
2 eggs
2 Tbsp. red food coloring
1 cup buttermilk

1 tsp. vinegar
2 cups flour
1 tsp. vanilla
1 tsp. baking powder
1 tsp. salt
1 tsp. baking soda
1 tsp. cocoa

Preheat oven to 350°.

Beat oil, sugar, and eggs together until well-blended. Add next four liquid ingredients, mixing well. Add dry ingredients and beat another 2 minutes. Bake in greased Bundt pan for 25-35 minutes, or until center springs back when lightly touched. Two 8-inch round cake pans may be used instead of a Bundt pan, if desired, decreasing the baking time by about 5 minutes.

Cool completely, and then frost.

Frosting for Red Cake

6 Tbsp. flour
1½ cups milk
1½ cups butter (not margarine)
1½ cups sugar
1½ tsp. vanilla

Cook flour and milk over medium heat, stirring until thick and smooth. Cool in refrigerator, stirring occasionally. Meanwhile, cream butter, sugar, and vanilla together. Add cooled milk mixture, beating 10-12 minutes until thick and creamy.

SUGAR

FLOUR

The Refrigerator

There's no better time for giving the refrigerator a good spring cleaning than now! While you're at it, consider rearranging the contents to make better sense for your daily needs. If you have those handy adjustable shelves, why not make them work for you instead of against you. A couple of hints:

Top Shelves:

· Items children seldom use
· Soft drinks and other beverages
· Leftovers (at eye level)

Middle Shelves:

· Lunch-Box stuff
· Eggs
· Space for more leftovers!
· Thawing meats and poultry

Bottom Shelves:

· Healthy snacks such as cut-up veggies, yogurt, apple sauce, fruit
· Milk, fruit juice, iced water, tea
· Open box of baking soda (it really does absorb odors)

Middle Drawers:

· Lunch meats, breakfast meats, cheeses

Bottom Drawers:

· Fresh fruits
· Fresh vegetables

Side Door:

· Condiments
· Sauces
· Dressings
· Pickles
· Jams and jellies

Notes

S·U·M·M·E·R

"Summer is here
when the chair you're sitting on
gets up when you do."

Unknown

Light Spinach Dip

Mix all ingredients together and chill. Serve with vegetables or baked crackers or chips.

1 (10 oz.) pkg. frozen chopped spinach, thawed and squeezed dry

1 cup light mayonnaise

1 cup light sour cream

½ cup fresh cilantro, chopped (parsley may be substituted here)

¼ cup green onion, minced

½ tsp. basil

½ tsp. ground marjoram

1 (1 oz.) pkg. buttermilk salad dressing mix (such as Hidden Valley)

Miniature Pork Kebabs

- 1 lb. lean pork tenderloin, cut into 1" cubes

- fresh vegetables, cut into 1-inch chunks (broccoli, onion, tomatoes, mushrooms are good choices)

- 1½ cups Marinade (see page 45), reserving ½ cup for basting

Marinate pork for 8-24 hours. Drain and discard marinade. Thread pork cubes onto small skewers, alternately with vegetable chunks. Grill (or broil) until well-browned, basting with reserved marinade. Serves 6.

"In the Pink" Lemonade

Mix well in a 2 quart pitcher:

1 cup lemon juice

1 cup sugar

6 cups cold water

a few drops of red food coloring

fruit for garnish (optional)

Chill until ready to serve.

For the most enjoyable lemonade experience, pour into frosty clear glasses and garnish with a sliced lemon and a fresh strawberry or cherry.

Makes 6-8 servings.

Lemonade Stand Tips
from Blake and Brooke

Anyone who ever had a lemonade stand as a child knows how much fun it can be, just for a day, to "set up business." When my children were small, they called their business "In the Pink, Inc." As in many areas of life, half the fun is in the anticipation and planning. Blake and Brooke share a things-to-do list to help you get ready for business. By the way, these basic rules apply to starting a grown up business, too.

1. Ask permission of all the right people and make sure you understand the rules.

2. Name your company.

3. Make some business cards. They can be made one at a time, out of construction paper decorated with markers. Or you can create them on the computer.

4. Make a shopping list. Extra things to give your product "added value" should be on the list. In the Pink, Inc. gives each customer a free sugar wafer with the purchase of a lemonade.

5. Make a budget and set a price for your product.

6. Make a sign.

7. Plan together now to divide the duties of running the business before you ever talk to your first customer. Discuss this plan with someone who has had experience in the business.

8. Have fun!

Shopping List

- 1 bottle lemon juice
- sugar
- red food coloring
- 4 lemons
- 1 jar maraschino cherries
- 1 package pink sugar wafers
- 1 package straws
- 20 large plastic cups
- 1 bag ice

Garlic Smashed Potatoes

6 Tbsp. butter
4 cloves of garlic, peeled
1½ lbs. Idaho potatoes, peeled and
   cut into eighths
1 cup of milk or half-and-half
salt and pepper to taste

Melt half the butter in a small saucepan over low heat. Add garlic cloves. Cover and cook until golden and tender, (about 20 minutes), stirring occasionally. Transfer mixture to a food processor and purée.

Cover potatoes with salted water in a larger saucepan and boil over medium-high heat until tender. Drain. Mash potatoes with a potato masher or electric mixer. Add remaining butter, milk, garlic mixture, and seasonings. Beat until light and fluffy. Serve warm.

Makes 4 servings.

Perfect Harmony
FRUIT SALAD

Have you ever noticed how some foods just seem to work together like well-sung parts of a song? Try this "harmonious" combination of fruits and nuts for a refreshing treat.

1 banana, sliced

1 cup sliced strawberries, cleaned and hulled

1 cup fresh pineapple chunks, drained

1 peach, peeled and cut into chunks

1 cup broken pecans

Dollop each individual serving with a little whipped cream, if desired. Makes 6-8 servings.

"Happiness is when what you think, what you say, and what you do, are in Harmony."

MAHATMA GANDHI

Midnight Moon

POTATO 🌿 SALAD

My neighbor and I threw this together late one Friday night in anticipation of a dinner for 12 people the next evening. While the potatoes are roasting, enjoy a cup of tea out under the starry sky with a treasured friend or neighbor... By the way, if you don't intend to make this dish the night before and you want a new name for it, we thought "Roasted Potato Salad with Dill" might work for you (but we're sticking with Midnight Moon!).

3 lbs. small unpeeled new potatoes
(or small red or white potatoes if new
potatoes are not in season)

2 shallots, chopped
Kosher or Margarita salt
1 cup sour cream
2/3 cup mayonnaise
3/4 tsp. dried dill weed
3 green onions, minced
freshly ground black pepper

Preheat oven to 400°. Spray a large shallow baking dish with vegetable oil spray. Arrange scrubbed and pierced potatoes in a single layer in a baking dish. Scatter shallots and salt over all and bake until tender, about 45-60 minutes. Allow potatoes to cool slightly. Then slice and toss with dressing (made from remaining ingredients) while still warm. Chill several hours before serving.
Serves 12-15 people.

Herbed Rice Mix

This is a great staple to keep in the pantry. It also makes a nice gift when packaged in bags or jars tied with ribbon. Don't forget to include cooking directions on a card or label when giving as a gift.

1½ lbs. long grain rice
½ cup celery flakes
⅓ cup minced onion
¼ cup dried parsley
1 Tbsp. dried chives
1 tsp. tarragon
2 tsp. salt
1 tsp. freshly ground pepper

Combine all of the ingredients listed above and store in an airtight container. Makes about 20 servings.

Directions for preparing rice:

Bring 2⅔ cups water and 1 tablespoon butter or margarine to a boil. Add 1 cup rice mix. Reduce heat and simmer for 20 minutes. Remove from heat; let stand for 5 minutes or until liquid is absorbed. Fluff with a fork. Makes 4 servings.

Hint: For a little variety, add ½ cup frozen peas, sliced mushrooms, sliced almonds, or broccoli bits during last 5 minutes of cooking.

There's the Rub!

Try this barbecue rub on meat or poultry...

1 cup granulated sugar

¼ cup each:
- seasoned salt · paprika
- barbecue spice and · garlic salt

2 Tbsp. each:
- onion salt   · celery salt
- chili seasoning (not powder)
- ground pepper · lemon pepper

1 Tbsp. ground ginger
½ tsp. ground cayenne pepper

Mix all together and store in an airtight container. Sprinkle lightly on meat or poultry before grilling.

44

MARINADE
FOR BEEF OR PORK

We thank Daisy Isenberg for contributing this recipe. Try using it with the Miniature Pork Kebabs featured on page 37.

1 cup Karo syrup (dark or light)
1 (12 oz.) jar plum preserves or jam
½ cup soy sauce
⅔ cup chopped onion
2 cloves garlic, crushed or garlic powder to taste
2 tsp. ground ginger

Boil ingredients for 5 minutes in a saucepan. Reserve some marinade to use for basting meat while grilling or broiling. Reserved marinade is also great for dipping, or as a sauce with rice. Marinate meat 4-12 hours. Drain marinade and discard.

Makes about 2 cups.

Barbecue Sauce

This recipe of Dee Stoelting's is really "two for the price of one," since she has included instructions for making Lemon Vinegar. I can see Dee in her very efficient kitchen, making an extra bottle while preparing this sauce, and trimming it with a yellow gingham ribbon to share with a friend.

⅓ cup Lemon Vinegar (see next page)
2 Tbsp. sugar
1 Tbsp. mustard
½ tsp. pepper
1 tsp. salt
1 thick slice of lemon or 1 Tbsp. lemon juice
1 small onion, coarsely chopped
¼ cup butter or margarine
½ cup catsup
2 Tbsp. Worcestershire sauce

Mix all ingredients together in a sauce pan and bring to a boil. Reduce heat and simmer 15-20 minutes. Dee doubles the recipe and keeps it on hand in the refrigerator all summer.

Makes about 1½ cups.

Lemon Vinegar

Sterilize bottles. Slice 4-6 lemons ⅛-inch thick. You will be dividing the lemon slices between two bottles. Roll slices up and gently push down the neck of the bottle. Cover with white vinegar. Cork bottles.

Add vinegar to the bottles again 2-3 days later, filling to the top. Recork bottles.

Use in marinades, salad dressings, and sauces, refilling with white vinegar after each use. Dee suggests using for up to 2 months before discarding.

3 cups cooked celery
1 small onion, chopped
1 cup catsup
1½ cups Barbecue sauce, divided
1 cup water
2 Tbsp. vinegar
2 Tbsp. Worcestershire sauce
2 Tbsp. brown sugar
salt and pepper to taste
1 tsp. chili powder
½ tsp. garlic powder
1 boneless chuck roast
(3-4 lbs.), trimmed
hamburger buns

In a slow cooker, combine the first 11 ingredients, using only 1 cup of the barbecue sauce and reserving the rest. Mix well and add roast. Cover and cook on high for 6-7 hours or until tender.

Remove roast; cool. Shred meat and return to sauce; add reserved barbecue sauce, and heat through.

Use a slotted spoon to serve on buns.

Makes 12-14 servings.

Barbecue Beef Sandwiches

Easy Manicotti

24 oz. ricotta cheese
1/4 cup grated Parmesan cheese
1 egg
12-16 oz. manicotti, cooked and drained
according to package directions
1 (28 oz.) jar spaghetti sauce
1 Tbsp. minced, fresh parsley
or 1 tsp. dried parsley flakes

For filling, combine cheeses, egg, and
parsley. Spoon into a large zip-top bag. Cut
off bottom corner of bag and pipe cheese
filling into manicotti noodles. Pour half of
the spaghetti sauce into an ungreased
13 x 9 x 2-inch baking dish. Place noodles
over sauce; pour remaining sauce over top.
Cover and bake at 350° for 20 minutes. Uncover
and bake 20 minutes longer until heated
through. Sprinkle with more Parmesan cheese,
if desired. Serves 6.

Barbecue Chicken Pizza

Follow the recipe for Pizza Dough on page 144 Then add this spectacular combination of toppings to create a pizza that is highly addictive and thoroughly satisfying.

2-3 boneless, skinless chicken breasts
2 Tbsp. olive oil
1 cup of your favorite barbecue sauce
4 oz. shredded smoked Gouda cheese
2 cups shredded mozzarella cheese
½ small red onion, sliced into ⅛" pieces
2 Tbsp. chopped fresh cilantro

Cook chicken in olive oil over medium-high heat until just cooked, 5-6 minutes per side. Do not overcook. Cool slightly, then slice on the diagonal into thin slices. Coat with 3-4 tablespoons of the barbecue sauce and refrigerate! Preheat oven to 425°. Roll out pizza dough as per directions and place on baking stone or pan.

Spread ½ cup to ¾ cup barbecue sauce over prepared pizza dough. Sprinkle Gouda cheese evenly over the surface of the pizza. Sprinkle half the mozzarella cheese over the surface. Top with chicken pieces, and then onion. Sprinkle remaining mozzarella over top. Bake about 10-14 minutes, or until crust is crisp and golden and the cheese at the center is bubbly. Remove from oven and garnish with fresh cilantro.

Serves 3-4.

Mexicali Quiche

- Single deep-dish pie shell, unbaked
- 8 oz. pkg. shredded cheese (Mexican Blend)
- 1/4 cup sweet red pepper, chopped
- 4 oz. chopped green chilies
- margarita salt to taste
- 3/4 cup salsa
- freshly ground pepper to taste
- 4 eggs
- 1 1/2 cups half-and-half
- 1/4 cup chopped fresh Cilantro or parsley

Preheat oven to 400°. Fill pie shell with cheese, red pepper, chilies, and salsa. Season with salt and pepper. Top with Cilantro. In a medium-size bowl, beat eggs and half-and-half together. Pour over ingredients in the pie shell. Bake for 20 minutes at 400°, then reduce oven temperature to 325° and bake 20 minutes more, or until set. Serves 6.

Teriyaki Chicken Barbecue

What a festive change from the standard grilled fare! Five minutes of prep time in the morning allows the chicken to marinate all day before grilling that evening. Serve with wild rice. 6-8 servings.

1 cup soy sauce
½ cup honey
2 cloves garlic, crushed
optional: 2 tsp. cornstarch
   to make sauce
6-8 chicken breasts, skinned
   and boned
6-8 pineapple rings
6-8 red or green pepper
   rings
2 tsp. cornstarch

Pass the sauce!

Combine soy sauce, honey, and garlic. Reserve half of this marinade, covering the chicken with the rest. Refrigerate 6-10 hours. Drain marinade off chicken and discard. Cook chicken on the grill until almost done. Then place 1 breast, 1 slice of pineapple, and 1 pepper ring on top of a piece of foil. Spoon a small amount of reserved marinade on top. Seal foil and grill for 20 minutes more. You may make a sauce with reserved marinade by adding 2 tsp. cornstarch to it, stirring over medium heat until smooth and thickened slightly.

52

Pasta with Chicken and Squash

Serve this with a simple salad and perhaps a side dish of sugar snap peas... very satisfying!

1 small onion, chopped
1 garlic clove, minced
5 Tbsp. olive oil, divided
2 medium zucchini, julienned
2 medium yellow summer squash, julienned
salt and pepper
1 lb. boneless skinless chicken breasts, julienned

¼ tsp. each dried basil, marjoram, and rosemary
1 (16 oz.) package spiral pasta
2 cups half-and-half
1 Tbsp. butter or margarine
2 cups shredded Mexican cheese blend or cheddar cheese

In a large skillet, over medium heat, sauté onion and garlic in 3 tablespoons oil until onion is tender. Add squashes and cook until tender. Season with salt and pepper. Remove from heat and keep warm. Add remaining oil to skillet; cook chicken with herbs until juices run clear. While chicken is cooking, prepare pasta according to package directions. Sauce is prepared by combining half-and-half and butter in saucepan until butter melts. Then add cheese, stirring until cheese is melted. Place drained cooked pasta on a platter. Cover with cheese sauce. Top with chicken and squash and serve.

Makes 6-8 servings.

Blueberry Oat MUFFINS

1 cup flour
1 tsp. baking powder
½ tsp. baking soda
½ tsp. salt
1 cup rolled oats
2 eggs

1 cup sour cream
5 Tbsp. butter
1 cup brown sugar
1 cup fresh or frozen
   blueberries (no need to thaw)
2 Tbsp. sugar

Preheat oven to 375°. Line a 12- cup muffin tin with muffin-cup liners. Combine flour, baking powder, baking soda, salt, and oats in a small bowl. Set aside. In a large bowl, beat the eggs with the sour cream. Melt butter and brown sugar together and combine well with egg mixture. Fold in flour mixture and then blue-berries. Fill muffin cups ⅔ full and top each one with a sprinkling of sugar. Bake 18-20 minutes until golden brown. Cool for 5 minutes before removing from tin. Makes 1 dozen.

Blueberry-Orange Muffins

Follow recipe as above, but add 1 cup well-drained mandarin orange slices with the blueberries. Mix the zest from one navel orange, the juice from the same orange, and ⅓ cup sugar until sugar is dissolved. As soon as muffins are taken from the oven, pierce the tops 5 or 6 times with a toothpick, then brush orange glaze over the top of each muffin repeatedly, until all glaze is used up.

Strawberry Twisties

You'll notice lemon zest listed as one of the ingredients in this recipe. If you don't own a zester, why not invest in one? This handy little tool produces an ever-so-tiny shred of orange or lemon peel that can add a lift (like nothing else does) to an "old" recipe.

Combine sugar, yeast, and water in a mixing bowl and stir until yeast is dissolved. Add sour cream, oil, egg, salt, and baking soda, and mix until well-combined. Gradually add enough flour to make a stiff dough. Then turn onto a lightly floured board and knead until smooth and elastic, adding remaining flour as needed to prevent sticking. Knead dough a total of at least 7 to 8 minutes. Shape dough into a ball. Place in a lightly greased bowl, turning once to grease surface of the dough.

- 1 package quick-rising yeast
- ¼ cup warm water
- ¼ cup sugar
- ¾ cup sour cream, room temperature
- 2 Tbsp. vegetable oil
- 1 beaten egg, room temperature
- 1 tsp. salt
- pinch of baking soda
- 3½ to 4 cups all-purpose flour
- 1 tsp. lemon zest
- ½ cup strawberry jam or preserves

♥ ♥ ♥ ♥

Cover; let rise in a warm place till doubled (about 45 to 60 minutes). Punch dough down. Turn out onto a lightly floured surface. Cover and let rest 10 minutes. Preheat oven to 375°. Roll out into a 16 x 12-inch rectangle. Combine lemon zest and preserves and spread on half of the length of the rectangle. Fold dough over to make a 16 x 6-inch rectangle. Cut the dough crosswise into 1-inch wide strips. Twist each strip a few times and place on a greased baking sheet, leaving 1½ inches between strips. Cover and let rise 30 minutes. Bake for 10-13 minutes, or until golden. Prepare glaze and drizzle over twisties.

Powdered Sugar Glaze: Combine 1½ cups powdered sugar, 1 Tbsp. milk, and ½ tsp. vanilla. Mix until smooth.

Makes 14 to 16.

Sweet and Light
C O R N B R E A D

If they serve corn bread in heaven,
I think this is what it might taste
like. Please pass the honey butter.

1 small pkg. white cake mix
   (such as "Jiffy" brand)
2 small pkgs. corn bread mix
   (such as "Jiffy" brand)
3 eggs
2/3 cup milk
1/2 cup water

Preheat oven to 375°. Prepare white
cake mix according to the directions on
the box using a whole egg, rather than
just the egg white. In a separate and
larger bowl, prepare the cornbread mix
according to directions on the boxes.
Gently fold the prepared cake batter into
the prepared corn bread batter and spread
into a 9 x 13-inch pan that has been lightly
greased. Bake 18 to 22 minutes or until
golden brown.

Makes
about 10-12 servings...

Pear Zucchini Bread

2 cups chopped peeled pears
1 cup shredded zucchini
1 cup sugar
1 cup packed brown sugar
3 eggs, beaten
1 cup vegetable oil
1 Tbsp. vanilla extract

3 cups all-purpose flour
2 tsp. pumpkin pie
   spice
1 tsp. baking soda
½ tsp. baking powder
½ tsp. salt
¾ cup chopped pecans

Preheat oven to 350°. In a large bowl, combine the first seven ingredients. In a smaller bowl, mix flour, pumpkin pie spice, baking soda, baking powder, and salt until well blended, and add to egg mixture. Fold in pecans. Pour into two greased 8 x 4 x 2-inch loaf pans. Bake 50-60 minutes, or until a toothpick inserted in the center comes out clean.

Cool in pans for 10 minutes; remove to a wire rack to cool completely.

Makes 2 loaves.

Banana-Fana-Fo Cake

While preparing this recipe, I suggest you make a mental checklist of all the reasons you're happy the 70's are behind you. (If you were born after that, call your parents and ask them!) Perhaps, though, for old times' sake, you could sing a few bars of "The Name Game," using each of the ingredients in this recipe as a verse in the song.

Cake:

1 cup vegetable oil margarine, softened
2 cups sugar
3/4 cup milk
2 eggs, slightly beaten

2 tsp. baking soda
3 cups flour
4 overripe bananas, peeled and mashed

Preheat oven to 350°. Cream margarine and sugar together until light and fluffy. Add 2 Tbsp. milk; add eggs, dry ingredients, and remaining milk alternately. Beat thoroughly. Fold in bananas and pour into three 8-inch greased cake pans. Bake 23-28 minutes. Cool completely before frosting.

Orange Cream Cheese Icing:

8 oz. cream cheese, softened
1/2 cup butter, softened
1 1/2 lb. powdered sugar

zest of 1 navel orange
juice of 1 navel orange

Blend cream cheese and butter together. Add orange zest and juice and mix thoroughly. Gradually add powdered sugar, blending until smooth.

STRAWBERRY CREAM PIE

This pie is fun to prepare on a summer morning in anticipation of an evening barbecue. Other berries can be substituted if you like.

PASTRY:

1 cup flour
2 Tbsp. powdered sugar
½ cup butter, cut in pieces
pinch of salt

Preheat oven to 350°. Mix all ingredients together and pat into a buttered 9-inch pie plate. Prick crust in several places. Bake 12-15 minutes until light golden brown. Cool.

FILLING:

4 oz. cream cheese, softened
½ cup sugar
1 cup heavy cream, whipped until it holds soft peaks
1 Tbsp. fresh lemon juice

Whip together until thoroughly combined. Pour into cooled crust and chill 1 hour.

TOPPING:

1 qt. fresh strawberries, hulled
½ cup currant jelly, melted

Arrange berries, points up, on filling. Carefully paint the berries with the jelly. Chill 3 hours before serving.

Black Tie Cookies

This "black and white" cookie need not be saved for a formal affair. A chocolate lover's dream...

Preheat oven to 325°.

2 1/4 cups flour
1/2 cup cocoa
1/2 tsp. baking soda
1/4 tsp. salt
1 cup dark brown sugar

1 cup butter
3 eggs
2 tsp. vanilla
6 oz. semi-sweet chocolate chips
6 oz. white chocolate chips
3/4 cup granulated sugar

In a medium bowl, combine flour, cocoa, baking soda, and salt. Set aside. In a separate mixing bowl, cream together sugars and butter. Add eggs and vanilla and beat until smooth. Add flour mixture and chocolates, and blend until just combined. Drop by the tablespoonful onto an ungreased cookie sheet about 2 inches apart. Bake 12-15 minutes.

Cool slightly before transferring to a cool, flat surface. Makes about 4 dozen.

Hot Fudge Sauce

½ cup butter
2 cups sugar
14 oz. sweetened condensed milk
4 oz. unsweetened chocolate
16 large marshmallows

In the top of a double boiler, over medium heat, combine butter, sugar milk, and chocolate. Melt completely and mix well. Add marshmallows. Heat until melted. Mix well and serve hot. May be stored in refrigerator for up to 3 weeks.

Makes about 4 cups.

"Not what we have, but what we enjoy, constitutes our abundance."
~ ANONYMOUS

Mary Phyllis Macaroons

The use of the word "macaroon" in the title of this recipe is a bit of a misnomer, I have to admit. But "macaroon" sounds so good paired with my mother's name. The recipe *does* contain ingredients common to the traditional macaroons (coconut and almonds, which coincidentally are also found in one of my mother's favorite candy bars). In some of my favorite childhood memories, I see myself on a trek to the "confectionery" to buy my mother an Almond Joy bar. She had an incredible sweet tooth, and it was not unusual for her to send my sister, brother, or me off in search of a little something to satisfy it.

The journey to the small, family-owned food shop took us across a creek, through the woods, beyond a field of wildflowers, and back into "civilization" onto Tesson Ferry Road. Thank you for memories of independence and adventure, Mom. I hope this recipe, created for you, brings back sweet reflections of your freckle-face children, delivering candy bars, wildflowers, and unconditional love.

½ cup vegetable oil margarine

½ cup butter
¾ cup brown sugar
¾ cup sugar
1 tsp. vanilla
2 eggs
⅓ cup cocoa
2⅓ cups flour
1 tsp. baking soda
1 tsp. salt

3 Almond Joy bars, chilled and chopped into bite-size pieces
1 cup shredded coconut
1 (3 oz.) bag sliced or chopped almonds

Preheat oven to 350°. Cream together margarine, butter, both sugars, and vanilla. Add eggs and beat until creamy and well mixed. Stir in cocoa, flour, baking soda, and salt until blended. Fold in candy "bar" pieces, coconut, and almonds.

Drop by the heaping tablespoonful onto an ungreased cookie sheet and bake 10-12 minutes. Cookies should be "set" but not overbaked. Makes 3½ dozen.

"The happiness of the domestic fireside is the first boon of Heaven."
~Thomas Jefferson

How can one create a book about the company we keep without addressing the subject of family and friendship gatherings? Whether we are the ones to organize these blessed reunions, or one of the many participants, these occasions are like manna from heaven, and should be approached with a certain reverence mixed with joy. Here are just a few ideas to stimulate plans for meaningful and lively get-togethers.

Gatherings

Family Reunion Fun

Family reunions can become the glue that holds the spirit of a family together. Reunions celebrate the strength and love that sustains the family. We gather together to honor past generations and acknowledge the future we want to secure for those who will carry on after us. What might make those reunions a little more memorable?

1. **Do Your Homework**. There are several wonderful books that give step-by-step directions to planning unforgettable family reunions. If you are the one organizing the event, a book like this will be a great investment. There are also books available to help you locate long-lost relatives.

2. **Spread Out The Duties Among Several Family Members**. This is not only to save your sanity, but to insure you are capitalizing on the talents of the family members as a whole. Besides, who will carry on the family tradition if something happens to the one member who is responsible for all aspects of the gathering?

3. **Highlight The Children**. Consider the value of including the little ones in most of the activities. Perhaps a separate invitation addressed directly to the children would be in order, mentioning activities in which they will participate, and a copy of the family tree with their names highlighted on it. This would help them understand the big picture and the part they play in it.

4. **Design a Family Reunion T-Shirt.** Maybe there is an artist in the family who would take responsibility for creating a family crest, or a design specific to the year and place you are gathering. Not only will it make a wonderful sentimental souvenir, but worn at the reunion, it acts as a common denominator among you.

5. **Remember To Make "Fun" and "Flexible" the Operative Words Throughout the Event.** Take into consideration the varied needs of the group, ways to include new members of the family, and ways to pay homage to those who are not present.

Friendship Trips

We all know how critical strong friendships are to our daily lives, especially if we have few family connections. If you are separated by the miles from important friends, take time to plan "friendship trips" with them. Using some of the same guidelines as in planning a family reunion, you can strengthen the tie that binds these priceless relationships. Make it a memorable, magical event. And commit it to the realm of tradition. Whether you gather the third weekend in October each year or once every three years in May, promise this time to each other and hold that promise sacred.

Notes

A·U·T·U·M·N

The days are growing shorter... Tau

Time to Plant BULBS!

A·S·T·E·R

RAKE·RAKE·RAKE·RAKE·RAKE·RAKE

Acer Nigrum

PRUNUS

CELTIS

Chrysanthemum

JUGLANS CINEREA

Quercus Alba

Harvest Time

APPLES

"Autumn is a second spring
when every leaf is a flower."

Camus

Apricot-Bacon

APPETIZERS

12 slices bacon, cut in half
24 dried apricots
brown sugar

Partially cook bacon. Wrap
one-half slice around a folded apricot.
Secure with a toothpick. Roll lightly
in brown sugar. Place on cookie
sheet. Bake in preheated
350° oven for about
20 minutes, turning once
midway through baking time.
Drain on a paper towel and
serve immediately
—with duck sauce
or soy sauce.

Beautiful Brie

1 Tbsp. olive oil
1 onion, chopped
½ sweet red pepper, seeded and chopped
½ sweet yellow pepper, seeded and chopped
½ lb. fresh mushrooms, sliced
2 (10 oz.) pkgs. frozen chopped spinach,
    thawed and drained
1 lb. Brie, rind removed and cut into ¼" slices
salt to taste

Preheat oven to 350°. In a skillet over medium heat, sauté onion and peppers in olive oil until onion is translucent. Add mushrooms and sauté until soft. Remove from heat and add spinach. Place in ovenproof dish. Cover with Brie and bake about 10 minutes or until cheese melts. Serve with crackers.

Bacon Tomato Dip

1 lb. bacon, cooked crisp, & drained
3 large tomatoes, peeled,
   seeded, and chopped
1 cup mayonnaise
1 Tbsp. Dijon mustard
2 Tbsp. minced green onions
2 Tbsp. minced fresh parsley
3 drops Tabasco
freshly ground pepper to taste

Combine all ingredients in a food processor and process until chopped but not pureed. Adjust seasonings if needed and serve with fresh vegetables or crackers.

Makes 1½ - 2 cups.

Caramel Apple SALAD

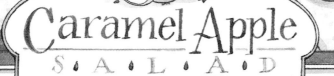

We thank Margi Whitworth for introducing this fun fruit salad to us! Don't let the unlikely list of ingredients scare you ~ they really do work well together. Because this salad looks a little bit like potato salad at first glance, you may want to garnish with some of those fun orange and chocolate sprinkles or chocolate curls to suggest the "dessertiness" of this dish.

1 (3.4 oz.) pkg. vanilla instant pudding

1 cup milk

1 (8 oz.) carton whipped topping
   (I used the fat-free kind)

6-8 Granny Smith apples,
   cored and cut into chunks

6 regular-size Snickers candy bars,
   cut into bite-size chunks

Fall-colored candy sprinkles
   or chocolate curls (optional)

Mix milk and pudding till blended. Fold in whipped topping. Add apples and candy bar pieces and mix well. Chill until ready to serve.

Serves 8-10.

Party Potatoes

This scrumptious dish will serve 15-20 of your closest friends (or family!). Boursin cheese may be purchased at most grocery stores, but if you have trouble finding it (as we do in our small town), there is a recipe for Boursin in _Just a Matter of Thyme_ (our first cookbook) on page 5.

2 (24 oz.) bags thawed frozen hash browns
2 onions, diced (about 3 cups)
2 cloves garlic, crushed
ground pepper to taste
1 lb. Gruyère, grated (not processed)
16 oz. Boursin cheese with herbs
1 cup half-and-half

Preheat oven to 375°. Grease a large roasting pan. In a very large mixing bowl, combine the potatoes, onions, garlic, and pepper with your hands. Mix in Gruyère and Boursin thoroughly. Boursin will be "clumpy", but don't worry; it will melt in the oven and spread throughout the dish.

Turn mixture into the greased roasting pan. Add extra freshly ground pepper, if desired. Pour half-and-half evenly over the top and bake, uncovered, for about 1 hour. Remove and stir from the bottom to distribute the browned potatoes. Return to the oven and brown for an additional 30-45 minutes.

Cindy's Corn Casserole

A special thanks to Cindy Lind for sharing this family recipe with us. Great with any main dish but especially nice with chili.

½ cup butter or margarine
1 can creamed corn
1 can corn, drained
2 small boxes corn muffin mix
1 16 oz. container sour cream

Preheat oven to 350°. Melt butter in a 2 quart casserole dish. Add remaining ingredients, mixing well. Bake 45-60 minutes, or until knife stuck in center comes out clean. Makes 6-8 servings.

Roasted Vegetable Medley

I predict you will love this recipe, not only because it tastes great, but also because it serves as a foundation for so many other dishes. Partnered with fish or poultry and rice, it rounds out a meal quite nicely. If there are any leftovers, try the bisque recipe on the facing page or simply toss the yummy veggies in an omelet or a quiche the next day.

Preheat oven to 350°. Spray a roasting pan or a large baking dish with vegetable oil spray. Spread vegetables in a single layer in the pan (not too crowded, please).

1 cup diced eggplant
1 medium zucchini, diced
1 baked potato, diced

2 tomatoes, in 1-inch chunks
1 onion, chopped
½ cup chopped red bell pepper

salt and pepper to taste

Spray combined vegetables with vegetable oil spray and season with salt and freshly ground pepper. Bake for 1 hour, stirring once after 30 minutes. Serves 6-8.

Roasted Vegetable Bisque

- 3-4 cups Roasted Vegetable Medley (see opposite page)
- 1 Tbsp. brown sugar
- 1 (28 oz.) can crushed tomatoes with roasted garlic and onion
- 1 pint half-and-half or heavy cream, reserving 1/4 cup
- 2 Tbsp. cornstarch

In a large skillet, combine crushed tomatoes and brown sugar with roasted vegetables and heat through. Meanwhile, in a large saucepan, heat 1 3/4 cup cream. Combine 1/4 cup reserved cream with cornstarch in a small lidded container and shake for about 30 seconds. Add cornstarch mixture to hot cream and stir with a wire whisk for about 5 minutes over medium-low heat until slightly thickened. Carefully stir in vegetables and serve!

Enough for 4 - 6 servings

rientange You Glad...

When I asked my sister, Jan, to name this recipe after she tasted it, her suggestion was the title you find here. If you are not familiar with this knock-knock joke, you must ask a child to share. One of my favorite qualities in my sister is her playful spirit. Her ability to keep things light and laugh at herself balances my tendency to be a bit too serious at times. While you make this fun bread, make a pledge to smile a little more often.

2 cups sugar
1 cup butter, room temperature
6 very ripe medium bananas,
    peeled and mashed
4 eggs, well beaten
1 Tbsp. fresh orange juice
2 tsp. freshly grated orange zest
2½ cups cake flour
2 tsp. baking soda
1 tsp. salt

... I Said "Banana" Bread

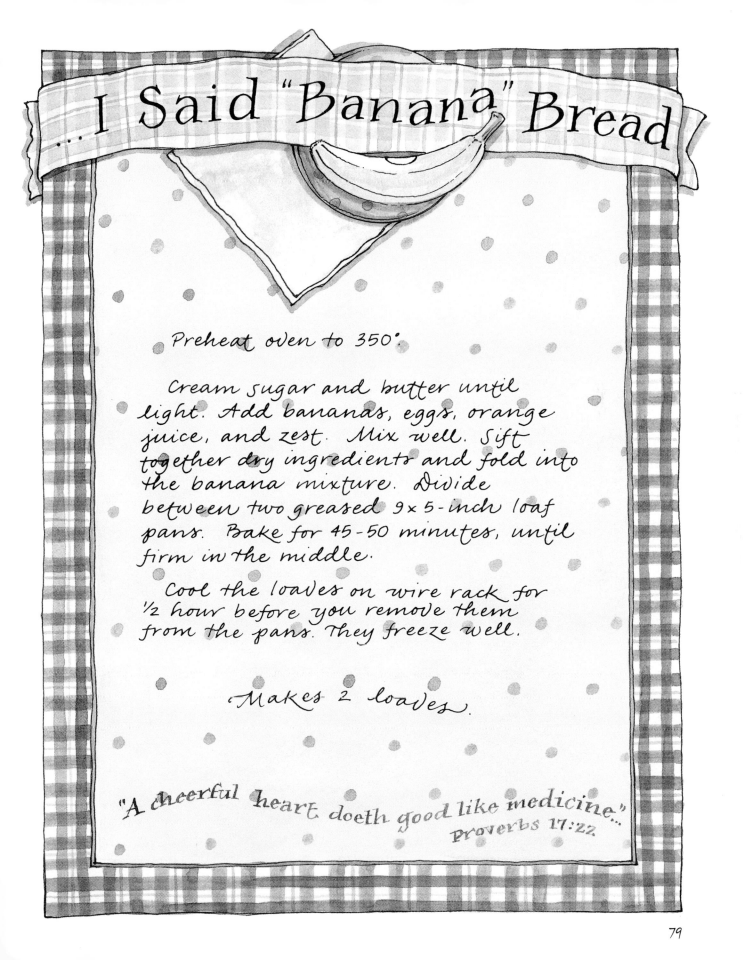

Preheat oven to 350°.

Cream sugar and butter until light. Add bananas, eggs, orange juice, and zest. Mix well. Sift together dry ingredients and fold into the banana mixture. Divide between two greased 9 x 5-inch loaf pans. Bake for 45-50 minutes, until firm in the middle.

Cool the loaves on wire rack for ½ hour before you remove them from the pans. They freeze well.

Makes 2 loaves.

"A cheerful heart doeth good like medicine..."
Proverbs 17:22

Create Your Own
M U F F I N S
♥

I enjoy including recipes like this one in our books because it takes some of the fear out of experimenting in the kitchen. Since flexibility is one of the key ingredients in remaining young at heart, it makes sense to introduce it into our daily routines whenever possible. Preparing this recipe will be one of those experiences where flexibility will give you immediate gratification.

3 cups flour
1 tsp. salt
2½ tsp. baking powder
1 tsp. ground cinnamon
¾ cup sugar, or a combination of
    white and brown sugar in this amount
½ cup butter or margarine, melted
    or 1½ cup vegetable oil
1 cup milk or cream or orange juice
2 eggs, beaten

Combine all dry ingredients. Combine all wet ingredients. Fold wet ingredients into dry and then add 1 cup of any **one** of the following and mix just until blended:

chopped nuts...

berries...

mashed bananas...

mashed pumpkin...

zucchini...

shredded carrots...

apples...

or applesauce.

Scoop into paper-lined muffin tins (fill about 2/3 full) and bake at 400° for 16-18 minutes or until golden brown.

Makes about 18 muffins.

Honey Orange Cream Cheese Spread

1 (8 oz.) pkg. cream cheese,
room temperature

⅓ cup honey
2 Tbsp. freshly grated orange peel
1 Tbsp. juice from the orange

Combine all ingredients in a bowl
and mix until smooth. Serve with
nutbread or muffins.

Harvest Muffins

You won't find a muffin with a richer autumn flavor than these!

2 cups flour
1 cup sugar
2 tsp. baking soda
1 tsp. cinnamon
½ tsp. allspice
dash of cloves
½ tsp. salt

3 eggs
½ cup vegetable oil
½ cup milk
1½ tsp. vanilla
1¾ cups chopped apples
1¾ cups grated carrots

½ cup chopped pecans

In a large bowl, combine first seven ingredients. In another bowl beat eggs; add oil, milk, and vanilla. Mix well and stir into dry ingredients until moistened. Fold in last three ingredients. Fill paper-lined muffin cups ⅔ full. Bake at 375° 18-20 minutes or until done. Makes about 18 muffins.

Sweet Potatoes Supreme

½ tsp. ground cinnamon
½ cup flour
½ cup firmly packed brown sugar
½ cup quick-cooking oatmeal
½ cup chopped pecans
½ cup butter, room temperature
2 (40 oz.) cans sweet potatoes, drained
2 cups fresh cranberries
2 cups peeled, cored, and sliced
cooking apples

• ♥ •

Preheat oven to 350°. Mix cinnamon, flour, brown sugar, oatmeal, pecans, and butter together until the mixture is crumbly. In a greased 2 quart casserole, layer half the sweet potatoes, half the cranberries, and half the apple slices. Sprinkle evenly with half the crumb mixture. Repeat the layers. Bake uncovered for 35 minutes, or until the top is lightly browned. Serves 6.

Hearty Vegetable Soup

Is there anything more satisfying than homemade vegetable soup on a brisk fall day? Combine these ingredients in a slow cooker before you leave the house, or cook in a stockpot on low for 1½ - 2 hours. Remove bay leaves. Served with hot biscuits or rolls, nothing could be finer.

3 Tbsp. vegetable oil
1 strip steak, cut into 1-inch cubes or 1 lb. stew meat (brown meat in oil before putting in slow cooker)

3 (10½ oz.) cans beef broth
3 cans water
1 (28 oz.) can crushed tomatoes
1 onion, peeled and chopped
3 carrots, peeled and cut into 1-inch pieces
3 potatoes, peeled and cut into 1-inch pieces
2 bay leaves
1 Tbsp. sugar
1 tsp. crushed sweet basil
seasoned salt and pepper to taste

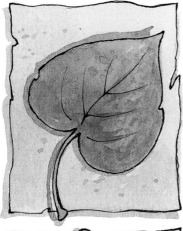

Makes 10-12 servings.

Corn Bisque

Pureed vegetables create the thickness for this soup, which makes it a bit healthier than traditional bisques. I did add a little half-n-half, I must admit. There are some tastes that just can't be compromised.

2 Tbsp. olive oil
½ cup finely diced green onions
1 small onion, finely diced
½ cup diced celery
2-3 Tbsp. flour
4 cups peeled and diced potatoes
4 cups frozen corn

6 cups chicken broth
2 bay leaves
1 Tbsp. Worcestershire sauce
2-3 drops Tabasco
1-2 tsp. seasoned salt
freshly ground pepper to taste
½ cup half-and-half

In a stockpot, heat olive oil over medium-high heat. Add both types of onions and celery. Cook, stirring constantly until onions are translucent. Sprinkle flour over potatoes and corn and cook for two more minutes. Add remaining ingredients, except half-and-half, and cook until potatoes are tender. Remove from heat and allow to cool slightly. Remove bay leaves and discard.

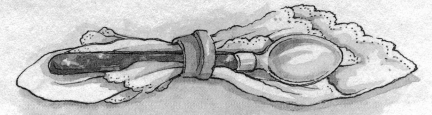

Transfer, 2 cups at a time, to a blender and puree until smooth. Return blended mixture to pot, stir in half-and-half, and gently heat through.

Makes 8-10 servings.

Wild Rice Soup

½ cup raw wild rice,
    rinsed and soaked according to pkg. directions
2 cups water
¼ cup butter
1 onion, chopped
3 carrots, peeled and chopped
½ cup chopped celery
1 cup chopped Canadian bacon
½ lb. fresh mushrooms, sliced
½ cup flour
3 (14½ oz.) cans chicken broth
1 tsp. dried snipped chives
1 cup half-and-half

Bring rice and water to a boil in a medium saucepan. Boil 45 minutes. Set aside. Melt butter in a large saucepan. Add onion, carrots, celery, Canadian bacon, and mushrooms. Sauté until vegetables are tender. Add flour and stir until liquid has evaporated. Slowly add chicken broth, whisking to blend thoroughly. Add wild rice and chives. Slowly add half-and-half. Heat through carefully and serve.

Makes 6-8 servings.

"Dinner,

a time when...
one should eat
wisely
but not too well,
and talk well
but
not too wisely."

W. Somerset Maugham

CHICKEN-CHILI STEW

1 onion, chopped
½ red pepper, diced
½ yellow pepper, diced
2 garlic cloves, minced
1 Tbsp. olive oil
3 chicken breasts, cooked and sliced into
    thin strips
1 (28 oz.) can diced tomatoes
1 (16 oz.) can pinto beans, drained and rinsed
1 (15½ oz.) can mild chili beans in chili sauce
    (I use Brooks)
1 cup mild salsa
½ pkg. chili seasoning mix
   or 1½ tsp. chili powder
   plus ½ tsp. ground cumin
1 (8 oz.) pkg. shredded Cheddar
    cheese for garnish

Sauté first 4 ingredients in oil until limp.
Add next 6 ingredients, mixing well. Bring to
a boil, then reduce heat and simmer for 20
minutes. Serve with cheese and tortilla chips
or corn bread.

Makes 6-8 servings.

Maurice's Hot Chicken Salad

Maurice McNabb was one of my first friends when I moved to Lake of the Ozarks to teach school back in the late 70's. Lucky for me, she was related to at least a few dozen people in town (or so it seemed), and I was made to feel like one of the family. Who knew then the influence Maurice (an art teacher) would have on the life of a 7th grade girl by the name of Shelly Reeves? We both thank Maurice for her quiet but mighty impact on our lives. This recipe is from a faculty cookbook the three of us put together twenty sweet years ago.

2 boneless chicken breasts, cut into bite-size pieces

¼ cup cornstarch

¼ cup vegetable oil

1 onion, peeled and sliced

¼ tsp. garlic salt

1 (4 oz.) can water chestnuts, drained

1 large ripe tomato, cut into chunks

4 oz. sliced mushrooms

¼ cup soy sauce

1 cup celery, sliced fried rice or Chinese noodles

Roll chicken in cornstarch. Fry in oil until tender. Sprinkle with garlic salt. Add remaining ingredients, except the last. Cover and simmer until vegetables are crisp-cooked. Serve over fried rice or Chinese noodles. Makes 4 servings.

Incredible Cavatini for a Crowd

This recipe will serve 12-15 people or it can be prepared in 3 separate casserole dishes, freezing the extra 2 dishes before baking. To serve the frozen dishes, thaw in the refrigerator the day before, then let stand at room temperature 30 minutes, and bake as directed below.

1 lb. ground beef
1 lb. medium or mild ground pork sausage
1 onion, chopped
8 oz. fresh mushrooms, sliced
1 (3½ oz.) package pepperoni slices, chopped
1 (28 oz.) can diced tomatoes with roasted garlic

1 (28 oz.) jar spaghetti sauce (I like
   the kind labeled "chunky vegetable")
1 (16 oz.) jar mild salsa
1 (16 oz.) pkg. shell macaroni, cooked
   and drained
1 cup grated Parmesan cheese
4 cups (16 oz.) shredded mozzarella
   cheese

   Cook ground beef, sausage, and onion
together until meat is done. Add sliced
mushrooms and sauté until mushrooms
are limp. Drain well; set aside.

   Combine the next five ingredients
with meat. Spoon half of this pasta
mixture into 2 lightly greased
11 x 7 x 1½-inch baking dishes; sprinkle
with half the Parmesan and
mozzarella cheeses. Top with
remaining pasta mixture. Bake
at 350° for 30 minutes; top
with remaining cheeses;
bake 5 minutes longer.

Dijon Pork Chops

We been hearing about Elaine's expert cooking skills from Anne, a mutual friend, for a long time now. Thanks for sharing, Elaine!

4 ½-inch-thick butterfly pork chops
6-7 Tbsp. flour
1 tsp. pepper
1 tsp. seasoning salt
½ tsp. poultry seasoning (optional)
¼ cup butter or margarine
2 Tbsp. finely chopped green onion
2 tsp. Dijon mustard
½ cup cold water
⅔ cup dry white wine
fresh chives to garnish

Pound pork chops with a meat mallet to ¼-inch thickness.

Combine 5 tablespoons flour with pepper, seasoning salt, and poultry seasoning in shallow dish. Melt butter in a large skillet over medium-high heat. Dredge chops in flour mixture and then brown in melted butter on both sides. Remove chops from skillet and set aside. Add green onion to skillet and cook until tender, about 1 minute. Stir together wine and mustard. Add to skillet and stir to combine with meat juices. Return chops to skillet.

Cover, reduce heat to low, and simmer 8-10 minutes or until tender.

Remove chops to warm platter.

Combine water and 1 tablespoon flour in a small bowl and mix well. Add to skillet and cook over medium-high heat, stirring constantly until thickened, about 1 minute.

Pour sauce over chops and garnish with chives before serving.

Makes 4 servings.

Turkey Tetrazzini

This recipe coincidentally comes from one of Maurice's cousins, Ann Roam. No matter how far away the Roam family roams (no pun intended), Ann and I have managed to stay close at heart. I have at least six different addresses for them in the directory I'm using now, and I think I've eaten this tetrazzini at most of those places.

1 to 2½ cups cooked diced turkey or chicken

1 (4 oz.) can mushrooms, undrained

1 Tbsp. minced dried onions

¼ tsp. Tabasco

¼ tsp. marjoram

1 (10¼ oz.) can cream of chicken soup

1 (13 oz.) can evaporated milk

1 (8 oz.) package spaghetti, broken into pieces, prepared according to package directions and rinsed under cold water

1 (4 oz.) package grated cheddar cheese

½ cup grated Parmesan cheese

Combine first seven ingredients and mix well. Divide spaghetti into 3 equal parts. Cover bottom of a greased 9 x 13-inch baking dish with layers of a third of the spaghetti, half the turkey mixture, and half the cheddar cheese; repeat, ending up with a layer of spaghetti. Sprinkle Parmesan cheese over top. Bake 30 minutes at 400° or until hot and bubbly.

Let set 10 minutes before serving. Can be made in advance. Serves 6-8.

Roasted Turkey

15 - 18 lb. fresh or frozen turkey*
salt and pepper to taste
1/4 cup butter, softened
stuffing recipe of your choice
3 ribs of celery, cut into large chunks
1 onion, quartered
1 oven roasting bag

Preheat oven to 325°. Sprinkle body cavity with a little salt and pepper. Loosely stuff neck cavity with stuffing. Fold skin over; secure with poultry pins. Stuff body cavity. Using pins, join skin; tie with string. Tie legs together. Rub butter, salt, and pepper over breast. Place turkey and vegetables inside roasting bag. Then place bag into roasting pan or onto a heavy baking sheet. Follow directions on roasting bag box for oven time in accordance to the weight of your turkey. Transfer turkey to carving board. Let stand 30 minutes. Remove stuffing to bowl and carve turkey. 12-16 servings.

* if frozen, thaw in refrigerator for three days.

What's in Your Heart

When I first started attending church as a young lady, I remember being nervous about being asked to pray out loud in front of others. My prayers seemed to lack elegance and order. "Practiced" prayers seemed somewhat insincere. A friend gave me some good advice:

"Just pray what's in your heart."

What's in our hearts on Thanksgiving day and everyday, I hope, is a gratefulness so deep and so true, that it practically leaves us speechless ~ but let's try anyway. Some families have a traditional blessing they share at mealtime that is passed on from one generation to the next. I like to think these prayers, though said countless times through the ages, never lose their power.

A Simple Family Blessing:

For the Hand that feeds us,
For the Heart that loves us,
For the Grace that saves us,
We give Thee thanks.

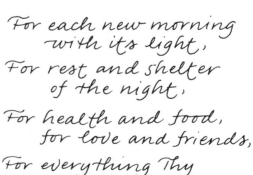

A Nursery School Prayer:

Thank you, God, this happy day,
for food and home
and friends
and
play.

For each new morning
with its light,
For rest and shelter
of the night,
For health and food,
for love and friends,
For everything Thy
goodness sends.

~ Ralph Waldo Emerson

Apple Pie Pockets

One of my daughter's favorite lunch box surprises... the prepared pie crust makes this recipe a cinch!

- 1 pkg. refrigerator pie crust
- 3 apples (peeled, cored, and sliced thin)
- ⅓ cup sugar
- 2 Tbsp. flour
- ½ tsp. cinnamon
- ½ tsp. nutmeg
- 2 Tbsp. butter
- milk
- ¼ cup sugar and ½ tsp. cinnamon combined in small bowl

fold

Preheat oven to 400° degrees. Cut each circle of pie crust into four wedges. Toss apple slices with flour mixture in a medium-size bowl. Place 6-8 mixture-coated apple slices on half of the pie crust wedge, dot with a bit of butter, and fold pie crust over top of apples. Seal around the open side edges with a fork dipped in milk. Slit top with a knife in a few places. Brush with a little milk and sprinkle with cinnamon-sugar mixture. Repeat with rest of pie crust pieces. Bake on waxed paper-lined cookie sheet until golden brown, or about 15-18 minutes. Great served warm with ice cream! Makes 8.

Easy Pumpkin Cheesecake

This recipe can be made in an 8-inch springform pan for a more traditional-looking cheesecake, using 1½ cups graham cracker crust crumbs mixed with 1 tablespoon sugar and 5 tablespoons butter (that has been melted) for the crust. Or you may follow the recipe below, using 2 "ready-made" graham cracker pie crusts for a quick and easy version.

2 prepared graham cracker pie crusts
3 (8 oz.) pkgs. cream cheese, softened
1 cup sugar
1 tsp. vanilla
1 cup canned pumpkin
3 eggs
½ tsp. cinnamon
¼ tsp. nutmeg
¼ tsp. allspice
whipped cream or non-dairy topping

Preheat oven to 350°. Combine cream cheese, sugar, and vanilla and mix well. Add pumpkin, eggs, and spices and beat until smooth and creamy. Pour the filling into the crust. Bake for 50-60 minutes or until set (60-70 minutes if using a springform pan). Cool to room temperature and then refrigerate. After cheesecake has chilled, serve with a generous portion of whipped cream on top. Serves 10-12.

Suzan's Fudge Nut Bars

Thanks to Suzan Carey for this scrumptious "brownie deluxe" recipe.

① Cream Together:
1 cup butter
2 cups packed brown sugar

② Mix in:
2 eggs
2 tsp. vanilla

③ In a separate bowl combine:
2½ cups flour
1 tsp. baking soda
1 tsp. salt
3 cups quick-cooking oats, uncooked

④ Combine dry ingredients with creamed mixture and set aside while you make the filling.

⑤ In a double boiler or microwave, melt:
12 oz. semisweet chocolate chips
1 cup sweetened condensed milk
2 Tbsp. butter
½ tsp. salt

⑥ Stir until mixture is smooth and add:
1 cup chopped nuts
2 tsp. vanilla

Spread about ⅔ oatmeal mixture in bottom of a greased 15½ x 10½ x 1-inch jelly roll pan. Cover with chocolate mixture. Dot with remainder of oatmeal mixture and swirl it over chocolate filling. Bake in a 350° oven for 25-30 minutes or until lightly browned.
Makes 60 (2 x 1-inch) bars.

Pineapple Raspberry Upside-Down Cake

6 Tbsp. butter
⅓ cup packed brown sugar
1 Tbsp. water
7 pineapple slices, drained
½ cup fresh or frozen raspberries
1 box yellow cake mix
   (batter prepared according to
      package directions)

Melt butter in a larger-than-usual round cake pan (9½ or 10-inches in diameter). Stir in brown sugar and water. Arrange pineapple slices on top of sugar mixture and fill in open spaces with raspberries. Prepare cake mix and spread evenly over batter. Bake at 350° for 30-35 minutes, or until a toothpick inserted near the center comes out clean. Cool on a wire rack for 5 minutes. Loosen sides and invert onto serving plate. Serve warm with whipped cream.

Makes 8-10 servings.

TAILGATE MARINADE

A special thanks to Lori and Greg Ranallo for sharing this recipe with us. As they are BIG Kansas City Chiefs fans and excellent cooks, we knew this would be a hit.

1 (32 oz.) can unsweetened pineapple juice
2½ cups sugar
1 tsp. garlic powder
3 Tbsp. white vinegar
2 cups sherry or 2 cups water

Mix all ingredients well. Pour enough marinade over chicken or steak to cover, reserving the rest for grilling (or it may be frozen). Refrigerate 48 hours.

Greg's grilling tip: After grilling the chicken or steak, garnish with grilled pineapple rings.

Apple Strudel

3/4 cup sugar

1/2 cup chopped walnuts (optional)

1/2 cup raisins, plumped in 2 Tbsp. water (optional)

1 1/2 tsp. cinnamon

2 lbs. tart cooking apples, peeled and sliced thin, (about 6 cups)

2 Tbsp. fresh lemon juice

1 cup butter, melted

1 lb. phyllo dough

2 cups cake crumbs or plain cookie crumbs (such as Vanilla Wafers)

powdered sugar

Combine sugar, walnuts, raisins, and cinnamon in a small bowl and set aside. In a larger bowl, toss apples with lemon juice to keep from turning brown. Add sugar mixture and combine gently. Preheat oven to 375°. Cover cookie sheet with waxed paper. Lay one layer of phyllo dough on the paper and brush with melted butter.

Sprinkle with crumbs. Repeat with 8 more sheets of phyllo. Place about 1½ cups of apple filling along narrow end of dough, leaving about 2½-inch margin at bottom and on both sides. Fold over margin and begin to roll strudel jelly-roll style. Do not roll too tightly, as dough expands during baking. Brush with melted butter. Cut 1½-inch slices about 1-inch deep, but not all the way through to the bottom.

Repeat with remaining strudel dough and apples ~ you should have enough for 3 or 4 strudels. Bake 35-40 minutes, brushing twice during baking. The strudel will be crisp and golden. Let cool slightly and serve warm with powdered sugar.

Note: Strudel can be assembled the day before, brushed with melted butter, and refrigerated. When butter is firm, cover completely with plastic wrap. To reheat leftover strudel, place in 300° oven for 10-15 minutes or until warm. Each strudel serves 4-6.

Packing Big Lunches for Little (and not-so-little) People

One of my favorite greeting cards in our store is published by Marcel Shurman. The front of the card pictures a worn-out woman with small children hanging from her every limb... The caption on the inside simply says: "It's been a long day with short people".

As challenging as those long days may be, wouldn't it be great if we could start off first thing in the morning feeling just a wee bit more organized and in control of the day's destiny? Packing lunches in the midst of the morning rush can be simplified a great deal by implementing some of these suggestions:

1. Keep two handled baskets, one for the refrigerator and one for the pantry, within easy reach of the little people. Fill them with lunch-boxable treats that can be grabbed in a moment's notice by even the smallest of hands.

Some Nice Choices:

· Fresh fruit and/or veggies (put individual zip-top bags inside the basket with grapes, carrot sticks, etc. in them)

Nice Choices, Cont'd...

- Individually wrapped peanut butter or cheese crackers
- Bags of chips or pretzels
- Beef Sticks
- Juice Boxes or bottled water
- Single-serving-size containers of pudding, yogurt, or canned fruit
- Cookies or brownies in individual zip-top bags

2. Send along a love note ~ if you can manage to sneak 30 seconds into your morning routine and also maneuver the note into the lunch bag unnoticed, you will no doubt lift someone's spirits by noon. We know of a mom who writes notes on her child's banana each day.

Other Tuck-In Ideas:

- Pretty Rocks (we have some in our store with messages engraved in them, but in the event you can't locate one of these "gems," try writing with a permanent marker on a smooth-surface stone).
- Coupons for dinner of your choice
- Small gift enclosure-size cards with your simple but sweet message.
- Small gift-wrapped school or office supplies (erasers, self-stick note pads, etc.)
- Treasure hunt clues or riddles

Notes

"Tis the season for kindling the fire of hospitality, the genial fire of charity in the heart."

Washington Irving

Spinach-Artichoke Dip

A slight twist on a famous restaurant chain appetizer — the presentation is especially nice during the holiday season but tastes great any time of year!

1 (14 oz.) can artichoke hearts, drained
1 cup grated Parmesan cheese
  (not in a shaker, please — use the real thing!
¼ cup chopped red bell pepper
1 cup real mayonnaise
1 (10 oz.) box frozen spinach, thawed and
  squeezed dry
1 clove garlic, minced
3 or 4 slices Monterey Jack cheese

1 jar of your favorite salsa
8 oz. sour cream
tortilla chips

Preheat oven to 350°. Coarsely chop artichoke hearts (a food processor makes this job easier) and blend in Parmesan cheese. Combine with the next four ingredients in a baking dish. Bake 20 minutes. Top with sliced cheese and return to the oven for an additional 2 or 3 minutes or until cheese is melted. Serve with salsa and sour cream on the side. Pass the chips. Serves 4-6.

Rothschild
Layered Sombrero Dip

The key ingredient in this appetizer is produced by Rothschild Berry Farm in Urbana, Ohio. Never will you find a more refreshing salsa than the one lovingly prepared by these people. If you can't find it in a specialty store near you, call them at 1-800-356-8933. They will be happy to share with you where you can purchase this and many more of their tasty treats.

Layer the following ingredients on a big platter. Serve with tortilla chips.

1¾ cups refried beans
1 cup diced green chiles
2 med. Avocados, ripe-cut into chunks
1½ cups Rothschild Berry Farm Garden Salsa
or Tropical Salsa
¼ cup sour cream
1 cup cheddar cheese, shredded
½ cup black olives, sliced
sliced green onions, optional
chopped tomatoes, optional

Gather the family around the table. Pull out some puzzles or games, put on some Christmas music, and dig in!

HOT·SPICED CIDER

1 quart apple cider
1 2-inch cinnamon stick
1 nutmeg, whole
3-4 cloves, whole
1 orange, sliced thin

Combine all ingredients in a saucepan and bring to a boil. Turn heat to low and simmer 5-10 minutes (the longer it simmers, the stronger the flavor). Strain, saving orange slices for garnish in each mug.
Makes 4-6 servings.

Hot White Chocolate

1 (2 oz.) top-quality white baking bar, chopped

¼ cup brewed coffee

1½ cups half-and-half _or_ milk

½ tsp. vanilla

a dash of ground nutmeg per serving

In a small heavy saucepan, melt baking bar over low heat. Stir in coffee, heat until smooth. Add half-and-half, cook over medium heat until hot. Do not boil. Remove from heat and stir in vanilla. Cool 5 minutes. Pour into blender and blend until frothy. Divide between two mugs. Sprinkle lightly with nutmeg.

Makes 2 servings.

Winter Fruit Salad

1 small box instant
  vanilla pudding mix
¼ cup pineapple juice
1 (8 oz.) container frozen
  whipped topping, thawed
1 cup pears, peeled and
  cubed
1 cup fresh pineapple
  chunks
1 cup sliced peaches
  (fresh or frozen and thawed)
1 cup seedless grapes,
  halved
1 cup dark, sweet cherries,
  drained

In a large bowl, combine
dry pudding mix and
pineapple juice. Gently fold
the whipped topping
into the pudding
mixture. Fold in
all fruits except
cherries. Cover
and chill for
up to 6 hours.
Just before serving,
add cherries.

Serves 6-8.

Baked Broccoli & Spinach

The magical combination of these two vegetables is wonderful. Served in a chafing dish, this could also double as an appetizer, served with tortilla chips or crackers.

- ½ cup butter
- ½ onion, chopped
- 3 Tbsp. flour
- 1 (10 oz.) pkg. frozen chopped spinach, cooked and drained
- 2 cups chopped raw broccoli (fresh is best!)
- 3 eggs, lightly beaten
- 2 cups small-curd cottage cheese
- 8 ozs. cheddar cheese, shredded
- salt and freshly ground pepper to taste

Preheat oven to 350°. Melt butter in a 7 x 11-inch baking dish. Add onion. Stir in flour. Combine spinach, broccoli, eggs, and cheeses. Season to your taste. Spoon vegetable-cheese mixture into onion mixture. Stir to combine. Bake uncovered 40 - 45 minutes.

NOTE To dress up this dish, remove dish from oven after 30 minutes, arrange sliced tomatoes on top, and sprinkle with Parmesan cheese. Return to oven for another 10-15 minutes. Serves 10-12.

Pam's Cranberry Salad

This dish is a holiday tradition in the May household, established by Pam. Each time I prepare it, I will think of Pam and what a difference she made in the lives of so many in our community. Thanks to her family for sharing this recipe, as well as the Forever Young Poppyseed Bread recipe on page 126

1 medium can crushed pineapple
1 can whole cranberry sauce
3 bananas, pureed in the blender
1 container of whipped topping
½ cup chopped nuts

Mix all ingredients. Pour into two loaf-size aluminum pans and freeze. Remove frozen loaf from pan when ready to serve and slice.

Makes 2 loaves.

Mrs. Chiles's
Cream Cheese Mashed Potatoes

Each of us has at least one someone special from our youth who made a tremendous difference in shaping our lives. If you clear your mind right now and think back to those days, I'm sure the sheer thought of that someone will warm your heart. Next to my own mother, no other person had a more meaningful place in my life than Mrs. Chiles. She shares with us this "comfort food," which is so fitting of her countenance. Prepare these not only as a special holiday dish, but any time you can see the benefits of giving just a little bit more of yourself than is required...

5 lbs. baking potatoes
8 oz. cream cheese
1 cup sour cream
2 tsp. onion salt

1 tsp. salt
¼ tsp. pepper
¼ - ½ cup butter
chives for garnish, if desired

Peel potatoes and cut into 1" cubes. Cook in boiling water to cover for about 15-20 minutes or until tender; drain and place into a large mixing bowl.

Add remaining ingredients; beat at medium speed with an electric mixer until smooth and fluffy (do not overbeat). Spoon into a lightly greased 3 qt baking dish. Bake at 350° for 30 minutes. Garnish with chives right before serving. 8-10 servings.

Note: Unbaked mashed potatoes may be chilled up to 2 days. Let stand at room temperature and bake as directed.

CHICKEN STRUDEL

Elegant and surprisingly simple, this makes a wonderful main dish for brunch. The filling can be prepared a day in advance, thawing the phyllo dough in the refrigerator at the same time. Serves 8.

3 whole chicken breasts, boned, cooked, skinned, finely chopped
1/4 cup finely chopped scallions
4 oz. fresh mushrooms, sliced
1/4 cup butter
1 tsp. garlic salt
1/4 tsp. Tarragon

1 Tbsp. Parsley flakes or 1/4 cup diced fresh parsley
4 eggs, beaten
freshly ground pepper
8 leaves phyllo dough
a small amount of melted butter
1/4 cup sliced almonds

Preheat oven to 375°. Sauté scallions and mushrooms in 1/4 cup butter until limp. Combine with chicken, seasonings, and eggs. On a large damp towel place 1 phyllo leaf. Brush with butter. Top with another leaf. Repeat until 4 leaves have been used.

Spread half of the chicken mixture down the center of the dough, leaving 1 inch at each end. Fold in the edges. Then roll up jelly-roll style. Place on buttered baking sheet, seam side down. Brush top with melted butter, and sprinkle with half of almonds. Repeat with remaining ingredients. Bake until golden brown, about 15-20 minutes. Slice and serve warm.

Honey-Spiced HOLIDAY HAM

You'll love the leftovers as much as the main dish!

10 lb. Ham (with bone)
½ cup honey
¼ cup butter
whole cloves

½ tsp. ground cinnamon
½ tsp. ground nutmeg
¼ tsp. allspice

Preheat oven to 350°. Place ham, fat side up, on a baking rack in a roasting pan. Score in a diamond pattern. Insert cloves into the center of each diamond. Bake, uncovered, about 2 hours. Combine all remaining ingredients and cook over medium heat. Stir until it comes to a boil. Spread this glaze over the ham and continue baking an additional 15 minutes.

Serves 12-14.

Mexican Chicken Casserole

This dish is a real hit with the children in our neighborhood. It's also great if you're planning a Mexican dinner buffet.

Serves 6-8.

Vegetable oil spray
1 pkg. corn tortillas
3-4 boneless chicken breasts,
    cooked and cut into small pieces
1 can cream of mushroom soup
1 can cream of chicken soup
1 can Rotel tomatoes, diced
1 (3 oz.) package cream cheese, room temperature
1 onion, peeled and chopped
½ cup sliced black olives (optional)
1 cup shredded cheddar cheese

Place ½ package corn tortillas in bottom of a 9 x 13-inch baking dish that has been sprayed with vegetable oil spray. Sprinkle half of chicken on tortillas. Mix soups, tomatoes and cream cheese. Pour half of soup mixture over tortillas and chicken. Repeat layer of tortillas, chicken, and with the rest soup mixture. Sprinkle with onion, olives, and cheddar cheese. Bake at 350° for about 20 minutes, or until thoroughly hot and cheese has melted.

Peppercorn Chicken Breasts

4 boneless, skinless chicken breast halves

1 Tbsp. freshly cracked pepper

1 Tbsp. butter

½ cup orange juice

½ cup cream

¼ tsp. dried tarragon

Place chicken between sheets of plastic wrap. Flatten to ¼" thickness using a meat mallet or rolling pin. Sprinkle with peppercorns. Melt butter in a large skillet over medium heat. Add chicken, cooking about 6 minutes on each side until chicken is done. Remove chicken and keep warm. Increase heat to high. Add juice to pan. Whisk in cream and tarragon. Boil, stirring constantly, until sauce is glossy and reduced to one-half its original volume. Spoon sauce over chicken and serve immediately.

Serves 3-4.

Cranberry-Orange MUFFINS

Rich and sweet, these muffins will become a favorite any time of year. Makes 6 jumbo or 8 medium size muffins.

1 ¾ cups flour
¾ cup sugar
2 ½ tsp. baking powder
¼ tsp. salt
¼ tsp. nutmeg
½ cup milk
⅓ cup butter, melted and cooled

1 egg, lightly beaten
1 tsp. vanilla
the zest and juice from one fresh orange, in separate bowls
½ cup (3 oz. pkg.) dried cranberries
½ cup sugar

Preheat oven to 400°. Grease muffin tin and set aside. Combine flour, sugar, baking powder, salt, and nutmeg in a large bowl. In a separate bowl, combine milk, melted butter, egg and vanilla, and half of the zest from the orange. Form a well in the middle of the dry mixture and pour in wet mixture. Gently stir until moistened. Fold in cranberries. Do not overmix. Fill each muffin cup ½ to ⅔ full. Bake immediately for 13 to 17 minutes or until lightly golden brown.

Meanwhile, make a glaze with remaining zest, ½ cup fresh orange juice, and ½ cup sugar. Bring this mixture to a boil in a small saucepan. Reduce heat and simmer about 5 minutes, stirring while glaze thickens.

Spoon glaze over muffins while warm... luscious with cream cheese   or butter!

Christmas Clam Chowder

While you may be concerned about how you will be able to stay awake long enough to complete all of the preparations for a fun Christmas Day with family and friends, you need not be concerned about what to serve for dinner that evening. This recipe will be like a gift you give to yourself during the hectic Holidays. It requires the most simple of ingredients and five minutes of your valuable time.

- 2 (10-¾ oz.) cans condensed New England Clam Chowder
- 1 (10-¾ oz.) can condensed cream of celery soup
- 1 (10-¾ oz.) can condensed cream of potato soup
- 2 pints Half 'n' Half
- snipped chives
- chopped red pepper or chopped tomato
- freshly ground pepper

Combine each of the condensed soups with the Half 'n' Half in a stock pot. Place oven on low heat, stirring often until heated through. After ladling soup in bowls, garnish with a sprinkling of chives and chopped red pepper or tomato for color, and season to taste with pepper. This chowder, served with warm muffins, makes a festive and tasty Christmas Eve supper. From our house to yours... Happy Holidays! Serves 6-8.

Broccoli, Beef & Noodle

SOUP

½ cup butter
1 onion, peeled and chopped
2 cloves garlic, minced
1 lb. stew meat, cut into bite-size
   pieces
¼ cup flour
6 (10 oz.) cans beef consommé
2 cups tomato juice
1 Tbsp. parsley flakes
1 tsp. crushed sweet basil
bay leaf
1 bunch broccoli, broken into
   small pieces
1 (8-oz.) package egg noodles

Melt butter in a stockpot over medium-high heat. Add onion and garlic and cook until onion is limp, stirring constantly. Add stew meat. Continue cooking meat, onion, and garlic until meat is lightly browned. Sprinkle flour over all, cooking and stirring for 2 minutes. Add one can beef consommé and stir for 2 minutes. Add remaining ingredients, with the exception of the egg noodles, stirring until well-mixed. Reduce heat to medium-low and simmer 30 minutes. Add noodles and simmer until noodles are tender. Serves 6-8.

Aren't these mittens by Bethany Lowe wonderful?

124

Walnut~Pear MUFFINS

Heather Berry,
(of Heart and Soul fame)
graces the pages of one of
our books again with this muffin recipe.
She recommends serving them with pear butter.

1½ cups white flour

⅔ cup firmly packed
brown sugar

½ cup whole wheat flour
(or increase white flour to
2 cups)

1 Tbsp. baking powder
½ tsp. salt
½ tsp. ground cinnamon
1¼ cups finely chopped and
peeled pear

⅓ cup coarsely chopped
walnuts, toasted

¾ cup low-fat milk

2 Tbsp. vegetable oil

1 large egg, slightly
beaten

cooking spray

1 Tbsp. granulated
sugar

Preheat oven to 400°. Combine first six ingredients
in a medium bowl; stir well. Add pear and
walnuts; toss gently to coat. Make a well in the
center of mixture. Combine milk, oil, and egg and
stir well. Add to flour mixture, stirring just until
moist (dough will be sticky).

Divide batter evenly among 12 muffin cups
coated with cooking spray; sprinkle with sugar. Bake
for 20 minutes, until a toothpick inserted in center
comes out clean. Remove muffins from pans
immediately; let cool on a wire rack. Makes 1 dozen.

"Forever Young"
POPPY SEED BREAD

I would like to imagine
Joey, Brett, and Julia dancing
to this song in the kitchen,
for many generations
to come.

3 cups flour
1½ tsp. salt
1½ tsp. baking powder
2¼ cups sugar
1½ Tbsp. poppy seeds
3 eggs
1½ cups milk
1 cup vegetable oil
½ tsp. each, Vanilla,
   almond, and butter
   extract

Combine dry ingredients. Add wet ingredients
and mix well. Bake in 2 large greased loaf
pans at 350° for 55-60 minutes.

Poke holes in bread
while warm and pour
glaze over top of each
loaf.

Glaze:

2 Tbsp. frozen orange juice
3/4 cup sugar
2 Tbsp. water
1/2 tsp. each:
    Vanilla, almond, and
    butter extract

"And may you be proud, dignified
and true... and do unto others
as you'd have done to you.
Be courageous, and be brave,
And in your heart,
you'll always stay
    Forever Young."

ROD STEWART

127

Chocolate Truffles

This easy recipe is so much fun because the end result is not just one type of tasty treat, but an assortment!

4 oz. semisweet chocolate, melted and cooled

3 oz. cream cheese, softened

1 2/3 cups powdered sugar

1/4 tsp. vanilla

Combine the above ingredients well and roll mixture into 3/4" balls. Then roll each ball in one of the following coatings:

Finely chopped nuts

Powdered sugar

Toasted Coconut

A mixture of 1/4 cup unsweetened cocoa, 2 tsp. powdered sugar and 1/4 tsp. ground cinnamon.

Place on a sheet of waxed paper in a single layer and refrigerate until firm. Makes about 2 dozen small candies.

P.S. These little sweets are great for your favorite Valentine or Easter Bunnies (just shape into "eggs" for this purpose).

Double Chocolate Drizzle Sticks

This is one of those magical recipes that requires only a few ingredients, very little prepararation, and even less clean up! Although we are using giant pretzel sticks as the "base" of this confection, you may get creative and try using strawberries, bananas, or pound cake in place of the pretzels. As a side note, this is a fun recipe to share with little ones.

YOU WILL NEED...

2 large zip-lock plastic bags
1 (12 oz.) bag white chocolate
    chips
1 (12 oz.) bag semi-sweet
    chocolate chips
1 bag jumbo size pretzel sticks

red and green
    candy sprinkles
coarsely chopped nuts,
    (if desired)
waxed paper spread
    on a cookie sheet

Empty each bag of chips into separate plastic zip lock bags. Seal tightly. One at a time, microwave on high for 1½ to 2 minutes. "Knead" bag gently to melt chips completely. Then cut off a tiny corner at the bottom of one side of the bag to create a pastry tube of sorts. Spread pretzels about 1" apart on the waxed-paper-covered cookie sheet. Begin drizzling chocolate back and forth across the top ⅔ of the stick. Repeat with the second kind of chocolate. Sprinkle with decoration of your choice. Refrigerate for about 30 minutes, or until set. Share with friends. Makes about 2 dozen.

Shaffer's Special Dessert

Linda Shaffer will always have a special place in my heart. Besides affording me the privilege of working with her two lovely daughters, she literally went the extra mile when she volunteered to help deliver over a thousand breakfast rolls to the capitol for the Secretary of State's Inaugural Breakfast (at 5 a.m.!) Enjoy this sweet treat that has become a Shaffer family favorite.

½ cup butter
1½ cups flour
¼ cup chopped pecans
12 ozs. cream cheese,
   room temperature
1½ cups powdered sugar
½ cup whipped topping

2 (3.4 oz.) packages instant
   French vanilla pudding
4 cups milk
whipped topping
pecan halves

Preheat oven to 375°. Melt butter in a 9 x 13-inch baking dish. Mix flour and pecans, and press evenly in bottom of baking dish. Bake this crust for 15 minutes, or until lightly browned. Set aside. Blend cream cheese, sugar, and topping, and spread this filling over cooled crust. Blend pudding mix with milk and pour over cream cheese mixture. Refrigerate for 5 minutes until set. Then top with whipped topping and pecan halves. Keep refrigerated. Serves 8-10.

Janice's Gingersnaps

I have to admit, I'm really picky about cookies. Not many bakers have passed the test of providing me with a cookie I can really get excited about. But Janice Steinmetz can bake for me anyday. Enjoy this recipe handed down by her mother (who received it from a college friend in 1951).

3/4 cup shortening
1 cup sugar
1 egg
4 Tbsp. molasses
2 cups flour
2 tsp. baking soda
1 tsp. salt
1 tsp. ginger
1 tsp. cinnamon
sugar for coating

Preheat oven to 350°. Cream shortening and sugar together. Add eggs and molasses. Mix well and add dry ingredients. Shape a generous tablespoon of dough into a ball and roll in sugar. Bake 8-10 minutes for chewy cookies or 10-15 minutes for crispy cookies. Makes about 36 cookies.

Four-Legged Family Member Treats

What would we do without the love and devotion of our family pets? Make up a stockingful of these treats for your dog or cat!

½ cup shredded cheddar cheese
½ cup shredded Parmesan cheese
3 Tbsp. vegetable oil
1½ cups flour (you may use part whole wheat flour)
¼ cup nonfat dry milk powder
2 tsp. salt _or_ garlic salt
½ cup water
cooking spray

In a large bowl, mix cheeses with oil. Stir in flour, milk powder, and salt until blended. Add water and knead until stiff yet pliable dough forms. Roll dough on a lightly floured surface to ¼-inch thickness, and cut out treats with cookie cutter. Gather scraps, reroll dough, and cut out more shapes, until all dough is used. Bake on lightly sprayed cookie sheets in a 350° oven for 25-35 minutes (depending on the size of the cookie cutter), turning once during baking. Treats should be golden brown when done. Let cool on wire rack.
Makes about 20-30 treats.

Friendship Soup Mix

Layer... this pretty soup (in order listed) in glass jars to give as gifts. Write out the directions for preparation in your own handwriting on a card or tag. Tie directions onto the jar, or place in a gift basket with some muffin mix. This list makes one batch.

½ cup dry split peas
⅓ cup beef bouillon granules
½ cup barley
½ cup dry lentils
⅓ cup dried minced onion
2 tsp. Italian seasoning
½ cup uncooked long grain or wild rice

Hint: If you will be making several batches of this mix, consider shopping at a bulk food store for some of the ingredients.

Other ingredients needed to prepare:

1 lb. stew meat
3 qts. water
1 (28 oz.) cans diced tomatoes

In a soup pot, brown beef, drain. Add the water, tomatoes, and soup mix; bring to a boil. Reduce heat; cover and simmer for 45-60 minutes or until peas, lentils, and barley are tender. Makes about 4 quarts of soup.

Tree Trimmings

ESTABLISHING TRADITIONS...

during the Holiday season can become such a meaningful part of the life you share with your friends and family. Many times those simple memories are the ones that bring us the most joy in the years to come. One of our family traditions involves decorating a miniature tree for each of the children's bedrooms. Tiny tree lights cast a soft glow on their faces, warming my heart, adding just a little bit of magic to each evening approaching Christmas.

TRY MAKING SOME CHRISTMAS ORNAMENTS TOGETHER, THIS YEAR...

An affordable batch of ornaments can be made by simply tracing with a soft lead pencil around the outside edge of cookie cutters onto bright scraps of fabric that have been "doubled" to create a front and a back. With right sides together, sew a 1/4" seam all the way around, leaving only a 1" opening for stuffing. Turn inside out and press with a hot iron. Stuff with poly-fiberfill and perhaps a little bit of potpourri. Stitch closed, attaching a pretty ribbon with which to hang the finished treasure from the tree.

Holiday Place Cards

Start a family tradition of allowing the youngest members of the family to create festive place cards for the holiday table. It will be fun to save them from year to year and watch how their artistic talents evolve as time passes. Here are a few simple ideas to get them started:

- Cut out small rectangles from construction paper and fold them in half so they stand up.

- Cut out a variety of holiday shapes from felt, play foam (found in the craft department), or colored paper. Glue these onto the construction paper. Add buttons, sequins, beads, or glitter.

- Don't forget to leave enough space to write names. Provide children with a list of printed names for them to copy onto the cards.

HOLIDAY NOTES

Morning, Noon, and Night

"We do not remember days,
we remember moments."
— Cesare Pavese

Morning Noon & Night

In each of our books we like to include a bonus chapter just for fun. It seems appropriate here to include some recipes that have become year-'round favorites.

I don't know if it's a coincidence, but many of the recipes in this section are also part of the little traditions within our families. Perhaps it has to do with the comfort quality of these foods. When my daughter, Brooke, was small enough to lounge in my lap, she used to say to me, "Mom, you're just so comfortable." She could not have paid me a higher compliment. We hope the recipes listed in this section are especially "comfortable" for you, your family and your guests. But mostly, we hope you find comfort _in each other_ morning, noon, and night.

♡ Our Keeping Good Company definition of "tradition" is a celebratory activity that puts love, comfort and meaning in your life, so that you do it again and again.

Cherry Almond Crumb Cake

- 1 cup flour
- 1/3 cup sugar
- dash salt
- 1/4 cup chilled butter, cut into small pieces
- 1/2 tsp. baking powder
- 1/4 tsp. baking soda
- 1/3 cup sour cream
- 2 Tbsp. milk
- 1 tsp. vanilla
- 1 egg
- 3 oz. cream cheese, softened
- 2 Tbsp. sugar
- 1 egg

- 1 cup cherry pie filling
- 1/4 cup sliced almonds

Preheat oven to 350°. Combine first three ingredients in a bowl and cut in butter until mixture resembles coarse meal. Reserve 1/2 cup of this crumb mixture and set aside. Combine remaining mixture with next six ingredients and beat at medium speed with mixture until blended. Spoon the batter into a greased 8-inch round cake pan. Combine cream cheese with 2 tablespoons sugar and egg. Beat until smooth. Spread evenly over batter. Dot with cherry pie filling and sprinkle with almonds and reserved crumb mixture. Bake 30 minutes or until cake springs back when touched lightly in the center. Cool on a wire rack.

Serves 8.

Janet's Breakfast Burritos

Thanks to Janet Bartels for this wonderful any-time-of-year breakfast dish.

1 lb. breakfast sausage
1 (15 oz.) can sliced white potatoes, drained and chopped

12 eggs
1 cup milk
½ tsp. cream of tartar (optional)
salt and pepper to taste
cooking spray
1 pkg. flour tortillas
2 cups shredded cheese (Mexican blend is good)
1 (16 oz.) jar salsa or picante sauce.

Serves 6.

Cook sausage until crumbly. Drain grease. Add potatoes to the cooked sausage. Simmer. Beat eggs, milk, and cream of tartar. Add this mixture to sausage and potatoes, season to taste, and cook to a scrambled-egg consistency. Preheat oven to 325°. Spray 9×13-inch pan with cooking spray. Fill each tortilla with egg and sausage mixture, adding some cheese to each tortilla before rolling burrito style. Place seam side down. Cover with salsa and top with remaining cheese. Bake 20 minutes.

CINNAMON ♥ BANANA WAKE-UP CAKE

⅓ cup butter, softened

1⅓ cups sugar

2 eggs

¼ cup water

2 bananas, coarsely mashed (not pureed)

1⅔ cups flour

1 tsp. baking powder

1 tsp. baking soda

2 tsp. cinnamon

¼ tsp. nutmeg

¼ tsp. ground cloves

½ cup chopped pecans

2 Tbsp. sugar mixed with ½ tsp. cinnamon

Preheat oven to 325°.

Beat together first four ingredients until well-blended. Stir in bananas and next six ingredients and mix well. Spread batter into a greased Bundt pan and sprinkle top with pecans, and cinnamon and sugar mixture. Bake for about 40 minutes, or until tester comes out clean. Allow to cool in pan.

Serves 8-10.

Cream Cheese Twists

If I had to name a favorite recipe in this book, this would definitely be one of the top ten contenders. You will be able to prepare these elegant pastries in less than 45 minutes, start to finish, but they will look and taste as if you were up since dawn. Prepare them for a special breakfast or make petite versions (half of the length described in these directions) for a brunch. They are best when eaten warm right out of the oven.

2 boxes (17¼ oz.) puff pastry sheets
(I use Pepperidge Farm)

8 ozs. cream cheese, room temperature

6 Tbsp. granulated sugar

1 egg

½ tsp. vanilla

1 tsp. cinnamon,
mixed with ½ cup granulated sugar

1 cup powdered sugar

1-2 Tbsp. milk
extra powdered sugar

♥

As you open the boxes of puff pastry, you will notice each sheet is folded into thirds. Lay each piece on a sheet of waxed paper to thaw before attempting to unfold dough. This will take about 20-30 minutes. Meanwhile, combine the cream cheese, 6 tablespoons sugar, egg, and vanilla. Mix until creamy.

Also take the time to mix powdered sugar and milk in a separate bowl, beating until smooth, to make a drizzly glaze.

Preheat oven to 400°. After the dough has thawed, gently unfold and cut each piece of dough where the fold lines are. Spread one piece of dough with ¼ cup of the cream cheese mixture, spreading all the way to the edge. Lay one of the other pieces of dough on top of the cream cheese.

Now cut lengthwise through both layers of dough and cream cheese filling every ½ inch, making 8 strips. Twist each strip twice and lay on a waxed paper-lined cookie sheet. Repeat with remaining dough until all 16 twists are lined up on 2 separate baking sheets.

Sprinkle twists lightly with cinnamon and sugar mixture. Refrigerate any remaining cream cheese filling in a covered dish. It will keep up to 2 weeks, and can be used as a surprise filling for brownies, muffins, nutbread, or coffeecakes. Bake twists 14-16 minutes or until light golden brown. Remove from baking sheets to cooling rack. Drizzle with glaze. Then sift powdered sugar over top of each.

Makes 16 twists.

Pizza Dough

1 tsp. quick-rising yeast
½ cup very warm water
1½ cups flour (¼ cup of which could be whole wheat flour)
2 tsp. sugar
1 tsp. salt
about ⅓ cup olive oil for total recipe

Dissolve yeast in a little warm water. Set aside for about 5 minutes. Meanwhile, mix together flour, sugar, and salt in a mixing bowl. Add 1 tablespoon of the olive oil, dissolved yeast, and the rest of the water. Mix by hand and knead about 5 minutes (you may lightly oil your hands to prevent sticking during kneading), or mix with electric mixer and flat paddle attachment for 2-3 minutes. Place lightly oiled dough ball in a greased bowl. Seal with plastic wrap and let dough rise in a warm place until doubled (about 45-60 minutes. Punch down and let rise again for about 30 minutes. Punch down a final time and divide into 2 equal parts.

Shape each part into a round "disk" and place on a pizza stone or pan that has been lightly oiled and dusted with cornmeal or flour. Gently push dough out to the edges of pan, forming a slight ridge around the edge. Now you are ready for the topping of your choice.

CHICKEN NOODLE SOUP

No household should be without a good basic chicken noodle soup recipe in the file. There are wonderful varieties created by simmering whole chickens, making your own stock and so on. But in a pinch, this shortcut will do nicely. Try this simple but satisfying version.

½ onion, peeled and diced

4 Tbsp. butter

6-8 boneless chicken breasts, cooked and diced

2 cups water

3 (14½ oz.) cans chicken broth

seasoned salt and pepper to taste

poultry seasoning to taste

1 tsp. crushed sweet basil

bay leaf

4 carrots, peeled and sliced

4 ribs celery, sliced

8 oz. frozen egg noodles

6 oz. sugar snap peas

Sauté onion in butter until limp. Add chicken pieces and cook an additional two minutes. Add remaining ingredients, with the exception of the noodles and the peas. Simmer 45 minutes, or until vegetables are tender. Add noodles and bring to a boil. Cook until noodles are tender. Add peas and heat through. Serves 8-10.

Best Baked Potatoes

For those of you who are skeptical about preparing baked potatoes in the microwave this recipe can be altered for oven use: simply bake in a 400° oven for 60-70 minutes, or until potatoes are tender in the center. But you really will be amazed at the quality of the microwave version, once you give it a try!

Scrub baking potato with a vegetable brush under running water. Pierce skin with a fork in several places. Spray baking dish with vegetable oil spray. Place potato in dish. Spray with vegetable oil spray. Sprinkle margarita or sea salt over sprayed surface of potato. Turn potato over and repeat with other side.

Cover dish and microwave for 4 minutes on high. Turn potato over and cook on high for another 3-4 minutes. Test for doneness. If fork slides easily into center of potato, it's done. If not, continue cooking, one additional minute at a time, until done. Add an extra two minutes of cooking time per extra potato in dish (2 potatoes - 10-12 minutes. 3 potatoes - 12-14 minutes, etc.)

Lowfat Toppings

- Butter Buds in place of real butter
- Reduced-fat cheese in moderate amounts
- Reduced-fat sour cream in moderate amounts
- Salsa
- Black bean salsa
- Steamed broccoli
- Chives
- Chopped onions
  - Hearty Vegetable Soup

Go-for-Broke Toppings

- Butter
- Chili
- Cheese
- Sour cream
- Bacon, cooked until crisp and crumbled
- Ham 'n' beans

Ham & Beans

Meat Loaf

Old fashioned comfort food
in one dish. Feel free to embellish
this recipe with your own special
touches.

1 lb. lean ground chuck
½ cup bread crumbs
1 Tbsp. instant minced onion
1 Tbsp. dried parsley flakes
1 Tbsp. dried celery flakes
1 Tbsp. Worcestershire sauce
1 tsp. salt
pepper to taste
2 Tbsp. catsup
1 egg
½ cup milk
cooking spray
2 slices bacon

Preheat oven to 350°. Combine ingredients, except for the bacon, in a mixing bowl (use your hands to mix together). Shape into a loaf and place in a lightly sprayed pan. Top with bacon and bake 45 minutes, or until done.

Makes 4-6 servings.

Options for the Top

- Before baking:
  glaze with 3/4 cup water and 2 tablespoons each vinegar, Dijon mustard, and brown sugar.
- After baking 35-40 minutes, "frost" with mashed potatoes, dot with butter, and return to oven for 15 minutes so potatoes are light golden brown
  - Douse with catsup before baking.

Grandma Roofener's HOT ROLLS

One of the first people I became acquainted with when I first moved from St. Louis to Camdenton, Missouri, at age 21 was Grandma Roofener. Everyone called her Grandma; it seemed as if she was everyone's grandma. I lived across the street in a little white house. Her house was the epicenter of activity in this little community. A variety of adults would lunch with her every Wednesday afternoon; a different group of children would show up in her yard after school each day. It was clear to me that love was drawing them near like a powerful magnet. Grandma drew me in too.

If I commented on her beautiful lilac bush, the next day there would be a glass jar filled with lilac blossoms on my porch with a handmade crocheted potholder under it: no note, but a warmer message could not be sent.

Thanks to Ann Roam (who first laid eyes on her husband when he was just a boy, climbing a tree in Grandma's yard), for sharing this time-honored recipe of her beloved Grandma Roofener.

A.K.A. Grandma Fener's Never Fail Hot Rolls

2 pkgs. yeast
1 tsp. sugar
2 cups warm water
2 tsp. salt
4 Tbsp. sugar
6 Tbsp. melted margarine or butter
6 cups flour

Empty yeast into a large mixing bowl. Add sugar and 1 cup water. Let stand for 10 minutes.

Then add to the yeast mixture the rest of the water, salt, sugar, margarine, and enough flour to make a stiff dough. Turn out on a floured board and knead for 3 minutes. Place in a well-greased bowl. Turn greased side up. Cover and let rise until double in size (1 to 1½ hours). Place dough on floured board. Pinch off pieces of dough about the size of a walnut and shape into smooth balls, placing them about 1-inch apart on greased baking sheet. Cover and let rise until doubled (about an hour). Bake in a 425° oven for about 20-25 minutes or until light golden brown.

Makes about 20 rolls.

Soft Pretzels

These pretzels have become a real favorite at our house!

1 (11 oz.) pop-can of refrigerated breadstick dough

vegetable oil cooking spray

about 1 cup vinegar in a shallow bowl

pretzel or margarita salt

melted butter (optional)

Preheat oven to 375°. Shape each piece of dough into a pretzel by making the half point of the dough the bottom point of a heart shape. Then bring both ends up and around to shape the top curves of a heart. Twist the two ends around each other once, then press the ends to each side of the bottom portion of the heart. Gently dip the pretzel shape in the bowl of vinegar, then place on a cookie sheet that has been sprayed with vegetable oil. Sprinkle with salt and bake until lightly browned, about 12-15 minutes. Brush lightly with melted butter, if desired, and eat while warm.

Makes 8 medium-size pretzels.

Cinnamon Strips

Great as a Mexican dinner appetizer, as a garnish alongside vanilla ice cream, or as a snack!

1 cup sugar
1 tsp. ground cinnamon
1/4 tsp. ground nutmeg
10 flour tortillas
cooking oil

In a large zip-top bag, combine sugar, cinnamon, and nutmeg; set aside. Cut tortillas into 3 × 2-inch strips. Heat 1-inch of oil in a skillet. When hot, fry 4-5 strips at a time until golden brown. Drain on paper towels. While still warm, place strips in sugar mixture in bag, shaking gently to coat. Serve immediately or store in airtight container.

Makes 4-5 dozen strips.

Dee's Kettle Corn

⅓ cup oil

½ cup sugar

½ cup popcorn

salt to taste

Heat oil and sugar in pan (make sure you have a lid that fits this pan before you start). Stir and add popcorn. Cover with lid and shake vigorously until popping stops. Spread on cookie sheet. Lightly salt.

Break apart when cool enough to handle. Eat warm.

Makes 4 quarts.

154

Simple Pleasures Poundcake

Janet Baker shares this recipe, handed down to her by her grandmother. Once you've made it and tasted it, you'll appreciate the name: its simple ingredients are a breeze to throw together, and its flavor is pure pleasure. Try topping each slice with fruit and whipped cream as embellishment.

1 cup butter

2 cups sugar

4 large eggs

1 tsp. rum extract

2 cups flour

powdered sugar, (optional)

Preheat oven to 325°. Cream together the butter and the sugar. Add eggs, one at a time, beating well after each addition. Add flavoring. Carefully add flour and mix well. Turn batter into a lightly greased Bundt pan and bake about 1 hour. Dust with powdered sugar if you like.

Note: I have also tried making little cupcakes with this recipe; it makes about 24. They can be frozen in zip-top bags and taken out one at a time for lunch box treats, or an impromptu midnight snack!

Serves about 12.

♥

HAPPY ♥ POPS

My children named these fun treats. In our community we are sometimes allowed to take snacks to school for mini-birthday celebrations for our children. Happy Pops are as much fun to make as they are to eat and have become my room-mother treat tradition for Blake and Brooke.

♥ 1 bag giant marshmallows, or enough for each child in the class to have a double pop (two on a stick)

♥ 1 (12 oz.) bag semisweet chocolate chips

♥ candy sprinkles (and/or chopped nuts or coconut)

♥ long sucker sticks (available in the cake decorating section of most discount department stores or in craft stores), one per child in the class and extras for teachers, principal, school nurse, and so on.

Lay a few sheets of waxed paper on top of baking sheets. Melt chocolate chips in a glass bowl in the microwave on high, or in the top of a double boiler. If you are using a microwave, heat for 30 seconds at a time, stirring after each 30 seconds, being careful not to scorch. It should not take more than two minutes to melt.

Run a sucker stick through the center of two marshmallows, stacked one on top of the other, so the stick does not go all the way through the top of the top marshmallow (much like a sucker in appearance). Dip* the marshmallow on the stick into the melted chocolate and sprinkle immediately with candy sprinkles, (or cover with chopped nuts or toasted coconut for the teacher treat!) We like to use "themed" sprinkles for different holidays. Lay the coated pop on the waxed paper to dry. Be sure to keep these in a cool place until you are ready to serve them. If they are bagged in cellophane bags (available at party stores), and tied with a ribbon, they make wonderful bake sale treats, too.

♥ You may decide spreading the melted chocolate on with a knife, instead of dipping it, is easier.

"Let us believe that God is in all our simple deeds, and learn to find Him there."
— A. W. Tozer —

Connie's Almost Fat-Free Chocolate Cake

1 (18¼ oz.) box fat-free
   devils' food cake mix
1 (14 oz.) can fat-free
   sweetened condensed milk
1 (12 oz.) bottle fat-free
   caramel ice cream topping

1 (8 oz.) container fat-free
   whipped topping
2 butter-brickle
   candy bars,
   crushed (Connie
   uses "Heath" bars)

   For best results, prepare cake one day ahead. Bake cake in 9 x 13-inch greased pan according to package directions. Let cool completely. With a wooden spoon, poke a dozen or so holes in the cake.
   Pour sweetened condensed milk over top of cake. Let soak for five minutes. Pour ice cream topping over cake. Let sit an additional five minutes. Frost cake with whipped topping. Sprinkle with crushed candy bars. Chill overnight. Makes 16 servings.

"May the Lord make your love increase and overflow for each other." 1 Thess. 3:12

"How do we get to where we
want to go
and still remain
a hero
to those we love?"

— Roger Staubach

*former Dallas Cowboys
Quarterback
Pro Football Hall of Fame*

160

We thank you...

once again for your interest in our books and for sharing them with your friends. It has been a geniune pleasure bringing these recipes to you, and we sincerely hope you will find them to be both fun and functional.

Some of the most heartwarming moments in the preparation of this book come when we were handling a few traditional recipe cards filled with the familiar handwriting of old friends who are no longer with us. These cards were written by the same hands that held the babies, wiped away tears—the hands that reached out to touch the lives of so many. We ache to hold the hands of these dear friends again. Their work here is done, but our hope is that each one of us will understand and embrace what work is left for us to do, and what kind of difference we are supposed to make in the lives of those we touch.

God bless you and the company you keep,

Shelly Reeves Smith
and Roxie Kelley

In loving memory of Grandma Roofener, Linda Shaffer, and Pam May

Substitutions for Common Ingredients

ITEM	QUANTITY	SUBSTITUTION
Allspice	1 teaspoon	1/2 teaspoon cinnamon plus 1/8 teaspoon ground cloves
Baking powder	1 teaspoon	1/4 teaspoon baking soda plus 5/6 teaspoon cream of tartar
Bread crumbs, dry	1/4 cup	1 slice bread, toasted and crumbled
Bread crumbs, soft	1/2 cup	1 slice bread
Buttermilk	1 cup	1 cup plain yogurt
Chocolate, unsweetened	1 ounce	3 tablespoons cocoa plus 1 tablespoon butter
Cream, heavy	1 cup	3/4 cup milk plus 1/3 cup melted butter (not for whipping)
Cream, sour	1 cup	7/8 cup buttermilk or plain yogurt plus 3 tablespoons melted butter
Flour, all-purpose	1 cup	1 1/2 cups cake flour
Flour, cake	1 cup	1 cup minus 2 tablespoons sifted all-purpose flour
Flour, self-rising	1 cup	1 cup all-purpose flour plus 1 1/4 teaspoons baking powder plus 1/4 teaspoon salt
Garlic	1 small clove	1/8 teaspoon garlic powder or instant minced garlic
Herbs, dried	1/2 to 1 teaspoon	1 tablespoon fresh herbs, minced and packed
Honey	1 cup	1 1/4 cups sugar plus 1/2 cup liquid
Lemon juice	1 teaspoon	1/2 teaspoon vinegar works in some dishes, but not where true lemon flavor is desired
Lemon juice	1 lemon	3 tablespoons bottled
Mustard, prepared	1 tablespoon	1 teaspoon dry
Onion, chopped	1 small	1 tablespoon instant minced onion
Sugar	1 cup	1 cup firmly packed brown sugar or 1/2 cup honey
Tomatoes, canned	1 cup	1/2 cup tomato sauce plus 1/2 cup water or 1 1/3 cups

Index